THE FOOTBALL MANIFESTO
AND
CLUB HANDBOOK

BRINGING THE BEAUTIFUL

GAME TO THE PEOPLE

AND MAKING THE USA #1

IN THE WORLD

BY: ROBERT WILSON

COPYRIGHT © 2018

The Football Manifesto
and Club Handbook

Bringing the Beautiful Game
to the People and Making the
USA #1 in the World

First Edition

By Robert Wilson Copyright 2018

This book is provided as an information source only. The information herein is subject to change and any information alleged to be factual is based on research from public sources or private sources that may or may not be reliable. While the information has been verified to the greatest extent possible it is not information that should be used or depended on in any way to make a decision of any kind. The information herein is therefore subject to further investigation and possible qualification or outright dismissal as to its veracity. Nothing herein should be relied on to make any investment decision. Nor is this book in any form an offer of or a promise to sell securities now or in the future. Any statements about the future are merely speculative. Third party decisions based on the contents herein will in no way be the responsibility of the author or publisher.

ISBN-13: 978-0-692-11141-3

ACKNOWLEDGEMENTS

I want to thank Professor William J. Morgan of the University of Southern California, for having shown the way through the intellectual thicket to a clearing, that in turn served as the prime inspiration for this book – a book drafted for lay appeal and which will hopefully put into praxis the beauty of the theory he described.

I also want to thank Michael Murphy, the co-founder of The Esalen Institute, for having been from a Western perspective a pioneer in modern times, of scratching and then digging below the surface of the potential of the body, sports and the divine.

Last year (2017) was the 40th anniversary of Steven Spielberg's *Close Encounters of the Third Kind.* A scene from *Close Encounters* captures the spirit of this book. In the movie, Richard Dreyfuss has been possessed by a mental image, a vision of a mountain, but it is a mountain he has never seen. In the scene, Dreyfuss is standing in his front yard shovel-in-hand and proceeds in a maddening frenzy to dig up the yard and throw shovel-full after shovel-full of dirt through his front window directly into his living room. This is all done in front of the neighbors and his wife and kids who are in the living room watching aghast. Anything he can get his hands on, trash, the trash can, garbage, anything and everything goes into his living room, and he proceeds to build a scaled mud and junk version of the mountain that reaches to the ceiling. Sweating profusely, filthy and exhausted he stands back to take a look at his creation, and just then he sits down and turns towards the television, which at that very moment has a breaking news story and a "live shot" of the very mountain he has created.

For a long-time football and in particular the parameters of the vision for football in the USA that are captured in this book, have been an obsession of mine. Looking back on it, this obsession borders on and in some sense fully overlaps with the obsession that Richard Dreyfuss captured in that movie.

It is a strange sensation to feel and to know that we are infinitely small unimportant pieces in a much larger cosmic puzzle. In this context, I want to thank my aghast family – my wife Denise and my sons Gabriel and Leonardo for putting up with my obsession.

In addition, I want to thank Bill Frederick whose design thinking and execution around the theme of sports continues to inspire, John Steinert and S. Courtney Booker III., who weathered through early versions of the conceptual framework with me, and Mike Fleisch for demonstrating the power of the visual in structuring collaboration at scale.

There are others who deserve a warm thank you, but who must by request, remain anonymous.

DEDICATION

This book is dedicated to the tens of millions of
football fans in the USA and Canada (and around
the world) who long to be member-owners of the
football club they choose to support

and to

Stephen Hawking and Marielle Franco

PLAUSIBLE DENIAL

"**Plausible deniability** is the ability of people (typically senior officials in a formal or informal chain of command) to deny knowledge of or responsibility for any damnable actions committed by others in an organizational hierarchy because of a lack of evidence that can confirm their participation, even if they were personally involved in or at least willfully ignorant of the actions. In the case that illegal or otherwise disreputable and unpopular activities become public, high-ranking officials may deny any awareness of such acts to insulate themselves and shift blame onto the agents who carried out the acts, as they are confident that their doubters will be unable to prove otherwise. The lack of evidence to the contrary ostensibly makes the denial plausible, that is, credible, although sometimes it merely makes it unactionable. The term typically implies forethought, such as intentionally setting up the conditions to plausibly avoid responsibility for one's (future) actions or knowledge. In some organizations, legal doctrines such as command responsibility exist to hold major parties responsible for the actions of subordinates involved in heinous acts and nullify any legal protection that their denial of involvement would carry.

High-ranking officials in more typically Eastern cultures, such as Japan or Korea, are often expected to take full responsibility for improper actions by their subordinates. As an example, Japanese CEOs have made dramatic public apologies and even committed suicide when their companies have been dishonored in some way.

In politics and espionage, deniability refers to the ability of a powerful player or intelligence agency to pass the buck and avoid blowback by secretly arranging for an action to be taken on their behalf by a third party ostensibly unconnected with the major player. In political campaigns, plausible deniability enables candidates to stay clean and denounce third-party advertisements that use unethical approaches or potentially libelous innuendo.

In the US, plausible deniability is also a legal concept. It refers to lack of evidence proving an allegation. Standards of proof vary in civil and criminal cases. In civil cases, the standard of proof is "preponderance of the evidence" whereas in a criminal matter, the standard is "beyond a reasonable doubt". If an opponent cannot provide evidence for his allegation, one can plausibly deny the allegation even though it may be true.

Although plausible deniability has existed throughout history, that name for it was coined by the CIA in the early 1960s to describe the withholding of information from senior officials in order to protect them from repercussions in the event that illegal or unpopular activities by the CIA became public knowledge. The roots of the name go back to Harry Truman's national security council paper 10/2 of June 18, 1948, which defined "covert operations" as "...all activities (except as noted herein) which are conducted or sponsored by this Government against hostile foreign states or groups or in support of friendly foreign states or groups but which are so planned and executed that any US Government responsibility for them is not evident to unauthorized persons and that if uncovered the US Government can plausibly disclaim any responsibility for them." [1]

[1] Source: Wikipedia and Office of the Historian, Department of State. *National Security Council Directive on Office of Special Projects (NSC 10/2),* Washington, June 18, 1948.

TABLE OF CONTENTS

THE MISSION

"Uber, the world's largest taxi company, owns no vehicles. Facebook, the world's most popular media owner, creates no content. Alibaba, the most valuable retailer, has no inventory. And Airbnb, the world's largest accommodation provider, owns no real estate. Something interesting is happening."
--- Tom Goodwin

Sports in the United States occupy increasingly massive amounts of our leisure time. Sports serve in many cases as the metaphors of our lives. The evolution of society is in no small measure related to the evolution of sports.

Technology, a thing-in-and-of-itself, much more than any one person or group, is constantly and increasingly forcing us to deal day-in day-out with what we do not know and with what we do not understand – namely, with the Other and ideas.

Despite the attempt to build walls, despite the attempt to fear-monger, despite the attempt to separate us from one another, technology incessantly bridges the gaps.

In no other sphere of society is this bridging taking place at a greater breadth and depth than in the world of sports. In particular, no sport serves more as a global platform for this technology-driven connectivity than football (soccer).

Football and its global exchange of cultures, languages and experiences de-mystifies the threat of the Other and de-mystifies the threat of ideas. Technology, particularly mobile technology and social media, like the constancy of ocean waves hitting a beach, wears down divisions. Football, the beautiful game, comes with a core mission – to fully integrate the USA with the rest of the world.

The Football Manifesto is about realizing that core mission.

PREFACE

My first exposure to psychotherapy occurred in the late fall of 1982. I had a lingering depression that somehow had grown over the preceding months to occupy center stage in my daily life.

When I awoke it was there. Looking in the mirror while shaving and it was there. I noticed myself slipping into a malaise, a mental lethargy, an angst in the middle of a perfectly normal and otherwise beautiful day. There was a feeling that somehow I had let something very important, something full of meaning escape my grasp.

In the evenings with my then fiancé, I found myself unable to concentrate, losing the thread of the conversation, or finding myself unable to control my mind from wandering back to events of several months ago. What could be causing this?

It really made no sense. There was no logical explanation.

After several sessions, my therapist's conclusion was that she had seen this phenomenon repeatedly. She called it (in Portuguese) *O Síndrome da Copa.*

She said the simple explanation was that I still hadn't recovered from the 1982 World Cup. The pain of Brazil losing to Italy was still too fresh. The antidote she suggested was group therapy – getting together with other Brazilians who had suffered the same fate of witnessing the 3-2 loss in Spain and the end of the dream and more than that, the end of the spectacle, the end of the beauty.

She explained that the real loss, the most difficult thing to let go of, was not the loss itself, but the staggering reality that I, that we, would never see that team play again.

It was the beauty that we witnessed, that the world witnessed, and the self-reflection that that beauty created in each of us, a collective and wholesome narcissism that paradoxically flowed with its own telepathy between fans, that was, in some cosmic sense, gone.

That joy was not recoverable.

All I could remember, like spreading a personal enveloping fog with my hands, was the shock of what appears in a clearing dead ahead – the shock of why I needed therapy. I was an American living in Rio de Janeiro and I had fully assumed the pain of grieving of an entire nation.

What gets created around football – the lifestyle, the permanent connection to a football club, the rivalries between clubs, the details of club history, the personalities and talents on the field and off, the wearing of the jersey on game day (and non-game days), the deep and lasting camaraderie, the gloriousness of a conspiracy of emotions, creates a gestalt.

Football becomes far more than the sum of its parts.

Football takes being a fan to another ontological level.

So the task here is not an easy one.

The challenge is two-fold: first, to convey the substance of an experience that is not available in the United States of America, and second, to establish the mechanisms in the USA, legal, design-wise and technological, that will allow for what is now theoretical to be experienced, to be lived first-hand.

This, the first edition of The Football Manifesto, is about laying a foundation to understand the challenge in front of us to make the USA #1 in the world of football.

"Meditation is to the East, what Sports is to the West."
-- Michael Murphy, Co-founder, The Esalen Institute

From the Muddy Mississippi to Ipanema Beach

I was born and raised in St. Louis, Missouri.

If you were looking at St. Louis using Google Earth, you would see that there is a bulge immediately below the conjunction of where the Missouri River meets the Mississippi River. That bulge which extends its curvature to the right and downwards represents the continued descent of the Mississippi and is a bit like drawing half of the oval outline of an egg with the other half of the outline of the egg curving back upwards and representing the city of St. Louis' Western city limits and its separation from St. Louis County.

I lived in a part of town that was called the Black Belt. The Black Belt was in fact a conglomeration of neighborhoods that was situated roughly at the geographic midline of St. Louis. I am old enough to remember the United States of America's own special version of apartheid.

All people of African descent regardless of income or education lived there. Doctors and lawyers lived next door to school teachers, janitors, plumbers, garbage collectors and the unemployed. In those days, there was no sense or even concept of multi-culturalism – there were just white people and black people (often called Negroes).

In other parts of St. Louis, there were neighborhoods, restaurants, stores, movie theatres that were off limits to blacks. This changed over time of course, but from my child's perspective, the hustle and bustle and dynamism of the Black Belt, of what in essence was a township (in the most pejorative sense), was a paradise. Life was charged with activity and with meaning in the midst of oppression.

I will spare you those details – suffice it to say that like so many inner-city youth in that epoch a good portion of my time was spent playing sports.

Whether at school, at the park down the street, at the local YMCA or the vacant lot next door, there was a constant diet of baseball, basketball and American football.

Looking back on it, St. Louis was unique. That was because via St. Louis's Catholic school system, a fourth sport was in evidence – namely, football (soccer).

In St. Louis you could go from pre-school to a Ph.D. and not leave the Catholic school system. That was because in addition to the plethora of K through 12 Catholic schools scattered throughout the city and St. Louis County, after high school you could attend St. Louis University, one of the leading Catholic universities in the country.

The Catholic Church catered primarily but not exclusively to the large immigrant Italian and German populations of St. Louis, which had brought with them strong football traditions. Football received as much press coverage for local high school sports as did baseball, basketball and American football. The only difference was that football was not played in the Black Belt.

Even though I didn't play football, I was exposed to it from an early age. St. Louis University is still the NCAA all-time leader in Division I championships for football. In 1966, Pelé and his famed Santos squad played a friendly against a local professional team called the St. Louis Stars and I attended with my father.

The St. Louis lore surrounding the sport is based on this rarely mentioned connection to the Catholic Church and also on the regional and national football awards dating as far back as the 1890s and early 1900s. The St. Louis Soccer League (1907-1938) was the first professional football league in the United States. In the 20s and 30s St. Louis teams rose to national prominence.

St. Louis featured Raphael Tracey on the United States Men's National Team (USMNT) that took a third place finish at the first World Cup in 1930 in Uruguay. Bert Patenaude on that same squad was the first player in the history of the World Cup to score a hat-trick and he later played for the St. Louis Central Breweries team from 1934-38 and won the National Challenge Cup (the highest achievement possible in football then and now known as the Lamar Hunt U.S. Open Cup). The USMNT that upset England in the 1950 World Cup in Brazil, was composed of 5 players from St. Louis on the starting 11. A local team Kutis was so dominant locally and nationally that they were asked to play two qualifying round games as the USMNT for the 1958 World Cup qualifying rounds.

When I first arrived in Brazil in the late 1970s, Brazil was still governed by a military dictatorship. It was shortly after the 1978 World Cup in Argentina.

There were parallels to be drawn from the experience of apartheid in the St. Louis of my youth, and the repression imposed by the military in Brazil, but there was also something truly special about both the time and the place in which I landed, Rio de Janeiro.

What Rio and Brazil lacked then in certain freedoms that we take for granted in the United States, and what in particular Rio lacked in infrastructure, efficiency and economic dynamism, it made up for with spectacular natural beauty, gregarious people, music, the beach and football (the 2014 World Cup and the 2016 Olympics created massive infrastructure improvements).

The only analogy that comes to mind, is that Brazil has done for football, what the USA has done for basketball.

In my youth, there was a basketball court at the corner of Taylor Avenue and Page Boulevard. It was a decent full-court and kids from all over would come there to challenge themselves and anyone else brave enough to step on the court.

As I got older we would travel to other parts of the city to find the best competition.

Rio was like that with football in the late 1970s. I remain convinced to this day, that there were people playing pick-up football games in Rio, on the beach, in the favelas or at the park, who could walk on to the pitch anywhere and dominate. In fact, some professional players from Rio's local clubs would periodically show up to play on the beach, attracting hoards.

From my arrival in the late 1970s until 1982, Rio and Brazil generally, was a football mecca.

There were many places in the city of Rio to find pick-up games. A few of these places were the equivalent of Rucker Park in New York City, but for football. If you wanted to find a game at 3am on a weekday night you could find it.

The mixing of cultures and races in Brazil has created a DNA pool of magnificent talent.

In the late 1970s everyone wore their hair long – as a response to the hippie, student and war protest movements of the 60s and early 70s, as a response to and in solidarity with the Black Power movement in the United States, and finally in response to the military dictatorship, which had taken control of Brazil in 1964.

At the pick-up games, called *peladas*, the ball skills on display were simply beyond imagining. It was the first time I had seen the best athletes that Brazil was capable of producing play the preeminent sport of the country and the world.

In the tropical heat of summer the glistening shirtless bodies at maximum physical exertion were complemented by a spectrum of long hair and oversized afros. Couple this with impromptu groups of musicians on the side-lines with drums, tambourines and cuícas beating out samba rhythms and it was quite the scene.

Summer in Brazil begins in mid-December (when the schools close) and goes until Carnival, usually toward the end of February or possibly early March. At some point in that summer of 1978-1979, I attended my first professional football game.

Remembering Maracanã

I was born a Flamenguista (a person who supports the Clube de Regatas do Flamengo) I just didn't realize it until I arrived in Rio.

Flamengo is one of Brazil's and the world's great football clubs, but it shares the stage in Rio with three other globally recognized football powerhouses: Fluminense, Vasco da Gama and Botafogo (there are over a dozen other professional football clubs in the Rio de Janeiro metropolitan area).

Founded in 1895, as a rowing club (the sport of the elites in the late 1890s) it didn't play its first football game until 1912. Flamengo has the largest fan base in Latin America, estimated at 45 million, larger than the country of Argentina.

You have to remember the setting. I had only recently arrived. I spoke only a few words of Portuguese and was not at all conversant. What little I knew of Portuguese was directly due to the fact that I had studied Spanish in school and had traveled in Latin America prior to my arrival in Brazil.

My first real lessons in the Portuguese language were taken from an exemplary set of professors, who just so happened to be Flamengo supporters. We always met in the grandstand of legendary Maracanã stadium (Estádio Jornalista Mário Filho is the official name).

These professors came from all walks of life (some with shoes, some wearing beach sandals and some barefoot), but they had in common that they had memorized and would say in unison all of Flamengo's songs and chants, and they were quite expert in telling the referees the mistakes that they had made, using the most colorful language imaginable (words, phrases and songs which immediately enlarged my Portuguese vocabulary), and of course these same professors were quite good at telling the fans cheering for the opposing team who they in fact were and about where they should go. *Filho da puta!!!* (son-of-a-bitch), *Vai para a puta que te pariu!!! Vai tomar no cu!!!* (I'll leave those untranslated), and many other phrases and songs became my introduction to the beauty of the Portuguese language.

In those days, Maracanã's grandstand (called the *arquibancada*) had no seats (except for a particular section called the *cadeiras especiais*, which were situated at mid-field in the *arquibancada* but on only one side of the stadium, and whose ticket prices were beyond most commoner's reach).

Imagine a terrace of ever larger and tiered concentric circle concrete slabs, rising up 50 centimeters and then back at a 90 degree angle for about one meter and then up again 50 centimeters and then back again at a 90 degree angle for one meter, and keep repeating those tiered layers of the grandstand until you get to forty or fifty of them (maybe more) rising in a perfect site line to the pitch, which then was maintained at the maximum size possible under FIFA regulations (110 meters by 75 meters), with the grass perfectly manicured and the entire field of play surrounded by an oval-shaped waterless moat, which was far too wide for any fan to jump across (although many tried).

Underneath the grandstand there was another tiered ring surrounding the pitch which was an all-seating section, which amounted to another smaller grandstand ring and underneath that there was the *geral*, a standing-only section that like the other grandstand rings, circled around the entire circumference of the field.

The *geral* was affordable to practically anyone and it was from the *geral* that dozens of frustrating attempts to reach the pitch by jumping over the moat were made. In all the years that I frequented Maracanã I never saw anyone make it.

Maracanã was built for the 1950 World Cup. The final, which Brazil lost to Uruguay 2-1, was seen by a crowd of 199,854.

Maracanã was massive and yet it had the intimacy of a temple. It was in many ways a place of worship. Having followed the sport closely for nearly 40 years, I remain convinced that the pitch in Brazil is mystically connected to the earth via a series of uniquely situated power points. One of these power points sits exactly in the middle of the pitch at Maracanã. How else can you explain the miracles?

I don't mean the miracles of winning or losing (everyone prays to God before the game and believes that God wears your team's colors), I mean the combination of athletes with skill sets that are dumbfounding, working with a simple round ball that all too often defies the laws of physics.

Part of the experience of being at Maracanã was enhanced by the fact that there were no bad seats – the site lines were a design wonder because the stadium was constructed without pillars (or at least no visible ones).

In this period, from the late 1970s until 1982, Flamengo had a team for the ages, led by Zico, but with a supporting cast that was also knocking on the door of immortality.

The game that stands out for me more than any other in this era, was the final of the Brazilian National Championship between Flamengo and Atlético Mineiro (from Belo Horizonte in neighboring state Minas Gerais) in 1980.

Both teams were packed with talent (remember this was prior to 1982, a date we will get to shortly in terms of its importance for Brazilian and global football). Flamengo won 3-2, with a goal from Nunes in the closing minutes of the second half.

Imagine Maracanã's *arquibancada* with its concrete slabs rising one after another, filled to the brim. If you are sitting in the *arquibancada*, you have to imagine that the one meter space behind you on the same slab of concrete can hold another person if that person straddles you with open legs. To really pack them in, three people could be sandwiched behind each other. There was something about tens of thousands of people in totally acceptable physical contact exchanging conversation, reacting with abandon to what was happening on the pitch and in many cases I must add, listening to the game with portable transistor radios plastered to their ears – and with so many radios playing simultaneously they echoed and reverberated stadium-wide with the voice of these genius football narrators who brought what was already a spectacle to an emotional crescendo conveying every pass, every dribble and every goal with a skin-to-skin emotion that simply cannot be captured in words. Over 154,000 attended the final. I was there. No words. Unforgettable.

I should also mention that in those days, drums, congas, tambourines, horns and other musical instruments were allowed in the stadium. The constant beat, the rhythms, the dancing in the stands, was all part and parcel of the experience. Huge banners were on display prior to the game by the various independent fan groups (*torcidas*) of Flamengo and whoever the opposition was. Colored smoke flares (the kind used for ships at sea) along with periodic fireworks was the custom.

While that final between Flamengo and Atlético Mineiro was simply unreal and unique because of what was at stake (Flamengo went on to defeat Liverpool 3-0 the following year to win its first and only FIFA World Championship of Clubs title), there was also something truly special and arguably even more intense when Flamengo played one of its cross-town rivals.

Flamengo, Fluminense, Vasco da Gama and Botafogo have had their own share of incredible players and teams, and when they play each other for a state or national championship, Maracanã experiences an intensity with fans on opposite sides of the stadium in a balanced non-stop chorus of chants, songs and demands for their respective teams. Games between these rivals are called *clássicos*.

The closest thing in the United States to this Rio-based rivalry in football, is to harken back to the glory days of baseball when New York City had the Yankees, the Dodgers and the Giants in town. Imagine through some time-warping process of sticking the Mets into that equation and you have a notion of what Rio is like.

For a *clássico* many people wear their club jerseys during the week in preparation for the kick-off, which is usually on Sunday afternoon. I have been at Maracanã on such a Sunday, after a late morning and afternoon at the beach, with a game time start of 17:00, as the sun's rays begin to give the day a different kind of lighting, a tint that is a reminder that this world is still, beneath the structured grime of our civilization, magical.

After attending a number of games, I became more accustomed to game-time rituals in the *arquibancada*. Not surprisingly and as is the custom at many sporting events, beer is a common denominator, along with peanuts, popcorn, candy and various soft drinks that are sold while the game is in progress.

Beer in those days was served in a somewhat large waxed paper cup that could hold a half-liter of beer. There was no limit on how many beers you could buy, so you can imagine based on pre-game and game consumption spirits were running high. The waxed cups served several purposes after they were used.

At one game I attended the guy in front of me folded, squeezed and twisted the cup into a nice round ball. He then proceeded to throw the cup at the back of the head of the gentleman seated in the next row down immediately in front of him. Obviously, the guy that got hit turned around to see where the balled-up cup had come from. But imagine this – as he turns around the guy who through the cup in the first place also turns around to look up toward the rows behind him in an attempt to "find" the culprit, as do other people in his row, as if they had rehearsed this. They hadn't. It was somehow understood. It was difficult to suppress the laugher. Especially given the fact that everyone knew what was going on.

And then there is the other waxed cup technique, which involves carefully crunching the circumference of the cup inward to create a cone-like structure with an opening at the top, which you then carefully urinate into. Once full, you pinch the top of the cone together to close it ever so slightly, and then throw it on your fellow fans below you in the *arquibancada*. This is called *levando uma mijada* or taking a urine shower, which is considered by truly devoted followers to be the official and sacred baptism for having attended Maracanã. I remember like it was yesterday when I took the splashed sacrament. It was a badge of honor. I received numerous pats on the back as a kind of welcoming into an inner-circle, a public but nevertheless secret society, a football hazing of sorts.

Maracanã went through a complete overhaul for the 2014 World Cup, and it is now, in my opinion, no longer the same place, no longer the same palace, no longer the same place of worship.

The field was reduced to the standard World Cup dimension of 105 meters by 68 meters. The impact of this from my perspective as a fan was devastating.

Brazilians are artists. They take pride in the beauty they create on the field far more than any other country. It is what Brazilians call *futebol arte*. Historically, it was always better to be more beautiful than to win. And ideally true greatness was doing both simultaneously. Brazil's 1970 World Cup team is a great example of that principal.

The extra meters in field length and width in the old Maracanã, was like providing a ballerina with a larger stage. Maracanã is now an all-seater. The concrete slabs of the *arquibancada* are gone. Seating capacity is a fixed 78,838.

Globalization has a way of stealing the magic out of life. Which brings us to World Cup 1982.

Until 1982, Brazil was able to retain its football talent. What the NBA represented (and still represents) for the world's best and most attractive basketball, Brazil represented for football. The 1982 World Cup in Spain changed all of that.

World Cup 1982 – Futebol Arte v. Futebol Força

There are two games that stand out for me from World Cup 1982. Italy v. Argentina and Italy v. Brazil.

1982 was Maradona's World Cup debut. That World Cup was also the watershed moment for a dramatic change in global football in two ways.

First, after this World Cup the most talented players from Brazil and Argentina left for European clubs. This began the first mass migration of world-class football talent to Europe, a trend that has become the global norm.

Maradona was a genius and the Brazilian team was one of the most beautiful teams to ever be eliminated from the World Cup. Maradona was hacked (along with Argentina) out of the tournament. Brazil, in my opinion, was also hacked and fouled out of the tournament. The elimination per se was/is not the problem. It is the way they were eliminated that I have problems with.

Second, the rules of the game (as promoted by the International Football Association Board (IFAB) and enforced by FIFA) favor individuals and teams with less football skills. To be blunt, European players were allowed to foul more skilled players and teams from Latin America, as the only means to win the game. Do not misinterpret what I am saying. The fouls were legal and according to the Rules of the Game.

Football is a ball skills sport. The only legitimate analogy in global sports is basketball. Basketball skills are demonstrated on the court simply and only because the rules protect highly skilled players. Imagine if Michael Jordan had not been allowed to play because every time he touched the ball he was held, his forward progress was interrupted or he was tripped or worse pushed to the floor. In the NBA talent is allowed to flourish and talent is protected and encouraged.

In football, the only other globally dominant ball skills sport, the rules are applied in exactly the opposite fashion. The more skilled the player, the more the rules permit maximum flexibility in fouling that player, in interrupting that players momentum and in putting that player on the ground. Look at the films from the

1982 World Cup game between Italy and Argentina. Gentile would not let Maradona get off the ground. Nothing against Gentile. He did what he had to do, and what he did was perfectly legal according to the Rules of the Game. But these rules are structured to favor European footballers, particularly when they face better skilled players from Latin America. Unlike basketball, IFAB and FIFA do not protect the best skilled players.

This is the essence of the debate between *futebol arte* (think Maradona and Brazil in the 1982 World Cup) and *futebol força* (think Italy in 1982 and European teams generally).

Look at the films on YouTube from the 1982 World Cup. Maradona spent more time on the ground than he did standing in the game against Italy. Zico, Brazil's brilliant midfielder, literally had the shirt ripped off his back in the game against Italy. I repeat this is not a polemic against Italy or any player on the Italian side.

This has to do with tolerating an unfair rule regime and its enforcement against the best and highest skilled players in the game.

Football needs to implement an individual and team foul regime a lá the NBA. The game needs to be rebalanced in favor of ball skills and in favor of *futebol arte*.

Both Brazil and Argentina have literally changed the way they play to accommodate the IFAB's and FIFA's rules. This is the dark side of globalization and the dark side of football's commercialization. These rules as they stand are one of the keys to European global football hegemony. *Futebol força* has won. That is the European model. The 1982 World Cup was a turning point. [1]

As we think about the future of football in the USA, it is imperative to move the USA in the direction of *futebol arte*, and away from *futebol força* to the greatest extent possible. The USA should opt for beauty over utilitarianism. Art over brute force.

For a country that has contributed little if anything to the men's version of the beautiful game, the least we can do is to champion the beauty.

Why The Football Manifesto and Club Handbook is Necessary

The United States of America needs a goal. We need a challenge that is right on the edge of being impossible. We need something that will unite us by testing us to the limit. Becoming #1 in the world of football is that goal.

In the USA today, the current approach at the bottom of the football pyramid is not an all-inclusive paradigm for youth football development.

There are ample sectors of our society and deep pockets of talent that are either marginalized or being ignored.

At the professional level no team in Major League Soccer (MLS) is capable of competing day-in day-out in the first division of any top European league. MLS teams would be hard-pressed to maintain themselves in the major European league's second divisions.

We need to change that. First, our youth development pipeline needs to be restructured so that young people everywhere irrespective of race, creed, color, orientation or income feel empowered and inspired to pursue the goal of becoming #1 in the world. We need to create a new dream for them.

Second, that new dream must be embodied in a radically different conceptual framework for football in the United States.

After research the best model in terms of its adaptability, proof of concept and robustness to launch this new football idea in the USA is an adapted version of Germany's Bundesliga.

Following Germany's example, we are also putting forth the proposition that football fans should be empowered as member-owners of the football clubs they support.

This is the best way to revitalize youth football and to restructure the football pyramid in the USA.

Our immediate goal is to begin by creating in the USA a new professional league and sixteen new professional football clubs that can compete consistently on par with the top-tier football clubs from Europe and Latin America (the two dominant regions in the world of football). These new fan and community-owned and supported football clubs will reach down and be fully integrated with the youth pipeline.

This first edition of The Football Manifesto will describe in detail the nature of the challenge before us.

A second edition of The Football Manifesto is already being developed and it will formally launch the new league and clubs with a full introduction of the concept of fan and community ownership of football clubs, and an A to Z toolkit for fans and communities to structure, launch, manage and grow football clubs from the grassroots to the highest levels of professionalism on the field and off.

Join us in building a football culture in the USA and becoming #1 in the world!!!!

[1] The debate about *futebol arte* v. *futebol força* predates by decades the 1982 World Cup. Europe and Latin America, with a particular emphasis on Brazil, Argentina and Uruguay (between them holders of 9 World Cup Championships), have debated the rules, playing styles and comparative on-field abilities for over a century. Brazil won 3 of its 5 World Cup titles in a span of 12 years (1958-1970). Many members of

that so-called *golden generation* of talent were recruited by European clubs, but only a very few accepted. Prior to that and in addition, Alfredo DiStefano, one of the greatest players to not play in a World Cup competition left Argentina and became a European legend with Real Madrid in the 1950s. Even so, the conjunction of corporate sponsorships, global television coverage, lucrative contracts and on-field star power converged for the first time in the 1982 World Cup. That date is the triggering point of the mass migration of global talent to Europe and the true beginning of Europe as the center of the football world.

INTRODUCTION

The purpose of this book is to start a sustainable grassroots movement in the USA to take control of the sport of football and put it firmly and permanently in the hands of its fans.

There is no precedent for this in professional team sports in the USA (with the qualified exception of the Green Bay Packers, see below).

However, there are rich experiences from abroad, particularly in Europe and Latin America that provide proven business model successes to borrow from and adapt to the special circumstances of the USA (and Canada).

The Football Manifesto is a mix of theory and praxis. It is also a work in progress.

The pace and quality of that progress will depend in part, on you the reader/fan -- because I am asking you to be proactive. Based on the content herein, I want you, the grassroots football fan, to take steps (praxis) to assert your individual and collective power. And in the process help me help you.

Buying this book is of course the first step. This first edition of The Football Manifesto is the precursor to a full-blown A to Z toolkit to establish neighborhood, community, town and/or city and fan owned and controlled football clubs.

Your purchase of this book, your use of the hashtag (#TheFootballManifesto), your contributions to Patreon and your feedback, will go toward making this movement a reality.

The current three professional outdoor football leagues in the USA and Canada, Major League Soccer (MLS), Women's National Soccer League (NWSL) and the United Soccer League (USL), when coupled with amateur and adult football, along with the NCAA, high school and youth football represent the so-called football pyramid.

That football pyramid is dysfunctional and represents a mountain of jigsaw puzzle pieces.

This book is, amongst other things, an attempt to put all of those pieces together in a new format and bring some order to the chaos.

This effort to organize, discover patterns and then construct a new cohesive picture out of football's puzzle parts, is also an effort to revitalize the basic democratic impulses and community building tendencies in all of us.

It is ironic but also timely that this book and the challenge of football's future in the USA, is occurring in the era of fake news.

The most recent presidential elections were indicative of a general feeling independent of party affiliation or ideology that the system was and is "rigged."

What does this mean? It means that a very small group of monied, powerful self-interested people have hijacked our country to benefit themselves, and have done so to our detriment and pain, by literally buying our elected representatives and manipulating our government and its rules against us, the people.

This takeover has occurred at the local, state and federal level. Special interest groups control our democracy and our economy and we the people, suffer the consequences.

Lamentably, in microcosm, this is also the current state of football in the USA. A small group of monied, powerful self-interested people, control the sport and its direction and future potential, to the detriment of the vast majority of football fans everywhere.

In order to change a "rigged" system we must take action. However, taking action requires a thorough understanding of what it is we are up against.

The first step is to educate ourselves.

Education is the antidote to fake news.

In addition to a pedagogical role, this book will also and hopefully inspire you!

Educational tools, once understood and coupled with a new found inspiration at the neighborhood and community level, will set the stage for an individual and collective critical analysis, debate, collaboration and construction of a new football paradigm in the USA.

Grassroots football fans in the USA represent a sleeping army.

This is your wake-up call!!!

Grassroots Organizing

In addition to the aforementioned tools, this book will employ (at least at this beginning point) a classic organizational development model: first, we will describe the current state of football in the USA and globally; second, we will describe the ideal future state of football (the vision of the future); and third, we will describe the transition state or the strategy of getting from our current state to our future state/vision.

The latter phase, the transition state, will present an initial set of parameters for our nationwide grassroots organizing efforts.

We will also establish feedback mechanisms so that the best of your ideas become part of the fabric of this new vision for football in the USA.

Along with and prior to this current state, future state, transition state model, some historical and contemporary critical analysis will be applied, as part of the overall pedagogical framework.

From one very important perspective, this is an exercise in democracy.

It is a rekindling of our true democratic impulses – for we seek a football of the people, by the people and for the people.

We will go into some depth and analysis about the women's and men's game, and in particular the global accomplishments of the United States Women's National Team (USWNT), but our emphasis here will be the men's game, both at the professional, amateur and youth levels, as well as in the context of the United States Men's National Team (USMNT) and the FIFA Men's World Cup.

To those who feel that this may be a sexist or male chauvinist approach, please accept my apology but also please do not pre-judge the book until you have read and digested it. I am subscribing to an analysis that says, that only by fully identifying, analyzing and correcting the errors made in the men's game, can we elevate both the men and the women to the world-class status they deserve.

Again, and to reiterate, we are not ignoring the women's game, the accomplishments of the USWNT or the FIFA Women's World Cup, which like the men, also occurs every four years.

Football Facts

All we have are the facts.

These facts are public information.

There is no smoking gun. There is no e-mail trail that can serve as the basis for an indictment. There are no recorded conversations that can be used in a court of law. There has been no access to any FBI informants or to the subpoena power of the government. Nor has the dark net provided access to information beyond the public's purview.

Fortunately, in the course of several years of research, many people have volunteered their time, information and in some cases very unique perspective and experiences, strictly out of their concern for the game. In some cases these sources have occupied (or occupy) sensitive positions in the football pyramid hierarchy.

What has happened (and is happening) in the world of football in the USA is so simple, so blatant and in your face, that upon reflection the real question is why wasn't this seen before?

And more importantly, why wasn't something done about it?

For the better part of two years I maintained a blog that followed the sport of football in the USA, and this book is a compilation, refinement and more in-depth analysis of those blog posts.

In none of those blog posts, however, did I reach the conclusions reached here (although there were intimations). Even prior to blogging, I had my doubts and eventually suspicions, that what was happening in the USA (and Canada) with football was out of the ordinary.

I have concluded that what is happening, meaning the current state of football in the USA, is purposeful and intentional and part of a larger plan and strategy – and that nothing has been an accident or simply the product of bad business judgment.

My professional life has largely been focused on investments in the emerging markets.

In particular, I work in a field known as private equity (PE). PE means the raising of substantial sums of money (usually in the hundreds of millions and sometimes in the billions of dollars from institutional investors and high net worth individuals (HNWIs)) to buy (usually) controlling stakes in companies. In my particular case, these acquisitions were made in developing countries, often times via privatizations.

For many years I was based in New York City, and the investments were done on behalf of Citi in various emerging markets. A bit more than twenty years ago, Citi sent me to Brazil to establish a dedicated investment fund for that country's sale of state owned assets, and to make a long story short, I and my family have been in Brazil ever since.

All of these years, we have lived in Rio de Janeiro and as a consequence, I have been deeply embedded in a country that is one of the quintessential examples of a football culture. It is relevant to add as well, that a small fraction of the investment fund we raised in the late 1990s, was used to take a controlling stake in a then first division Brazilian football club.

That hands-on experience and exposure to Brazilian football culture, informs some of the perspective I am conveying with this book.

The business world can be a strange place. Company financials only tell part of the story. Sometimes things about a business are hidden, either inadvertently or on purpose by a seller or even a buyer. At some point in your career you begin to have a sixth sense about people and businesses. Certain things despite appearances don't add up. For me football in the USA was and is like that.

Admittedly, I have been outside of the USA for quite a while. This fact cuts both ways.

On the one hand, I have an intimate grasp of the country, the culture, the language and all of the nuances that entails. And being "outside" provides a unique set of objective lens.

On the other hand, not having been in-country for over two decades is a disadvantage, because I have been unable to witness first-hand the dramatic changes that the USA (and Canada) have gone through.

This is important. The USA is a very different country from the one I left. The population of the USA is now 325 million. In 1997 the population was 273 million, and in 1990, the population was 250 million.

In the last 20 years 52 million people were added to the roles. And since 1990, 75 million have been added.

Many of these new Americans came from overseas and/or were the children of immigrants, and in practically all cases these immigrant populations originated from nations with deep long-standing football cultures. [1]

This means that football in the USA and Canada is embedded in a culturally evolving complex demographic setting with legal, political and investment ramifications.

Globalization along with these demographic trends of increasing diversity in the USA, when woven into broader and deeper trends in technology, particularly mobile technology, create a special set of new unprecedented dynamics regarding football's future.

The Big Question

For purposes of this book, the simple and yet big question to begin with was – why is the richest country in the world not a dominant football power on the global stage?

This is particularly relevant when we recognize that every other major team sport in the USA (baseball, basketball, hockey and American football) represents respectively, the best professional league on the planet.

Over time, another question demanded to be asked. Namely, how are sports, and in particular and again, professional teams sports, used in the USA to manufacture consent, to guide consumerism and to control thinking, emotion and our values?

Is the commodification of sports in a capitalist society, simply a mechanism to maintain the status quo of non-critical thinking alienated consumerism?

Or from a cultural perspective is there a deeper and more profound analysis regarding professional team sports?

Can football and the culture that surrounds it, be used to raise consciousness? Can football be used to bring people together, and to keep them united in an awareness of the mutual ground of their individual and collective struggles to evolve healthier communities, regions and the nation itself?

The problem with this set of questions and any proposed answers or solutions, is that today in the USA, there is no *culture of football* and the football pyramid isn't simply in chaos – it is in direct conflict on several fronts.

To complicate matters even further, the people of the United States of America are disconnected from one another. The overall mood nationwide is unstable at best, and at worst, a potential tinderbox.

In truth, this disconnection starts of necessity with a disconnection from oneself. This fragmentation of one's self causes pain, and inevitably triggers separation from others, setting the stage for an *us* versus *them* mentality.

At the extreme, this disconnection leads to group balkanization and can cause great tension, distance and sometimes aggressive and even violent responses.

How our economic system and the powers that ultimately control it, foster this climate as a tool to maintain not only power but the status quo, is a key element that must figure into any solution for the beautiful game.

At this level of disconnectedness, life can feel empty, or worse, there can be a loss of feeling itself. This is often referred to as alienation – where life can feel less than real.

This kind of pain, resulting from fragmentation and disconnectedness, can be found as easily in rural and small town USA, as in our great urban centers or inner-city neighborhoods.

Football as a Healing Mechanism

"Sport has the power to change the world. It has the power to inspire, it has the power to unite people in a way that little else does. It speaks to youth in a language they understand. Sport can create hope, where once there was only despair. It is more powerful than governments in breaking down racial barriers. It laughs in the face of all types of discrimination."
--- Nelson Mandela

You have heard before that there is nothing more powerful than an idea whose time has come. Fan and community-owned football clubs is that idea. Football is more than a sport, it is a culture, and that culture captures aspects of our common humanity, our cooperative nature and our global connectedness.

Football can heal us. Football can bring us together.

Football can reconnect us to ourselves, to others and to the planet.

The Football Manifesto is about reconnecting at the local grassroots level, at the regional level and nationally. It is about having a set of goals that everyone can buy into.

It is about building something together. It is about rolling up your sleeves and becoming engaged. It is about waking up in the morning with a sense of purpose. It is about creating meaning in our lives.

It is also about being involved with the creation of a new set of shared individual and collective values. It is about recognizing the connection between work and love. It is about acknowledging that there is excellence and genius in each of us.

All of this is part of the exciting challenge that football faces in the USA.

However, and before anything else, we need to understand how football is being and has been manipulated in the USA to benefit special interest groups, and in particular special interest groups that do not have football as their number one priority.

In the USA the dominant model for professional team sports is exemplified by what will be referred to as the Big 4: the National Football League (NFL), Major League Baseball (MLB), the National Basketball Association (NBA) and the National Hockey League (NHL).

The National Collegiate Athletic Association (NCAA), high school and amateur sports organizations, and lower schools and youth organizations (some public and some private) serve as feeder mechanisms for the Big 4.

Collectively, the Big 4 generates roughly USD 25 billion a year in revenue. Those four professional leagues represent 123 teams. All 123 teams are owned by wealthy individuals or small groups of wealthy individuals.

The exception is the NFL's Green Bay Packers. The Green Bay Packers are a community-owned American football team.

The NFL has adopted a special rule for the Packers, allowing for full participation in the league in exchange for a ban against community involvement in team management and any other community-owned team joining the NFL. That ban has been applied *de facto* to the other members of the Big 4. The Packers remain the only community-owned team in professional team sports in the USA. [2]

To highlight this situation a bit further, not only do you have to be in the top 1/10 of 1% of the population in terms of wealth to own a professional sports team in the Big 4, but given the fact that only 123 teams exist, we can roughly estimate that less than 1000 people are the owners of a USD 25 billion industry.

To summarize and set the stage for the rest of the book, the Big 4 sports team ownership model, carries a number of "key" attributes:

first, and to reiterate, its emphasis is on wealthy individual owners for each franchise;

second, those four leagues represent the global standard of excellence – they are the best sports leagues in the world in their respective sport;

third, at the professional level, each league is a monopoly; and

fourth, the Big 4 have largely adopted a generic branding (and marketing) model for all 123 teams.

Given the Big 4, and given additional options like the NCAA, NASCAR, the WNBA, tennis, golf, videogames, NETFLIX (and Hollywood generally), not to mention Sirius XM Radio, network TV, cable, satellite, streaming, social media (e.g., Facebook, Twitter, Instagram, Amazon, Google, etc.) and dozens of other options, where does football fit in to the USA's entertainment and leisure-time landscape?

That is a question that has been addressed since the 1994 World Cup by the United States Soccer Federation (USSF or U.S. Soccer), and by Major League Soccer (MLS), which was founded in 1996.

This book will address the history of U.S. Soccer and MLS strategically, but before a deeper domestic focus on the challenges before us, we have to recognize the one outstanding fact that makes football unique as a global sport – the existence of the Fédération Internationale de Football Association (FIFA).

FIFA'S Role

FIFA is a private association headquartered in Switzerland that describes itself as an international governing body of football, futsal and beach football.

FIFA was created in Paris in 1904, and declared that while it was the global governing body for the sport, the actual and so-called Laws of the Game would be laid down by another organization, the International Football Association Board (IFAB).

IFAB was created in 1886. Because the modern version of the game of football originated in Great Britain, IFAB is represented by the four countries of the United Kingdom – England, Scotland, Wales and Northern Ireland.

Each U.K. association has one vote, while FIFA has four votes. Any changes in the Laws of the Game, however, require a 3/4 vote. This means that FIFA's support is necessary but not sufficient for a motion to pass. As of 2016, all members must be present for such a vote.

In this overall context, the questions to be dealt with are:

What is the current state of football in the USA and globally?

What is the future state or vision of football in the USA that we seek?

How do we transition from the current state of affairs to arrive at our future state/vision? What strategy or strategies will get us there?

That is the sum and substance of the remainder of this book.

[1] For instance, in my own home town of St. Louis, since having left to pursue my studies, the city has become the largest per capita presence of Bosnians outside of Bosnia-Herzegovina, with a population of approximately 75-80,000. They bring the beauty of the Islamic religion but also the deep football tradition that their former country, Yugoslavia was known for. With a population of 3.5 million, B-H qualified for the 2014 World Cup in Brazil. Their contribution to the sports landscape of Europe is radically disproportionate to the size of the population. Their presence in St. Louis reinforces an already sterling reputation for the city as a football mecca.

[2] The Packers have been a publicly owned, non-profit corporation since August 18, 1923. The corporation currently has 360,760 stockholders, who collectively

own 5,011,558 shares of stock after the last stock sale of 2011–2012. There have been five stock sales, in 1923, 1935, 1950, 1997, and 2011. Packer shareholders are not entitled to and do not receive any form of financial return on investment. For more see: http://www.packers.com/community/shareholders.html

According to the World Population Review, as of 2017, Green Bay, Wisconsin has a population of 105,000 in the city proper and 312,000 in the metro area. See: http://worldpopulationreview.com/us-cities/green-bay-population/

PART I: TOOLS FOR A CRITICAL ANALYSIS OF FOOTBALL IN THE USA (OR ANYWHERE)

"There is a cult of ignorance in the United States, and there has always been. The strain of anti-intellectualism has been a constant thread winding its way through our political and cultural life, nurtured by the false notion that democracy means that my ignorance is just as good as your knowledge."
--- Isaac Asimov

The following tools, described over the next several chapters, are theoretical and/or practical in their application. They will allow you to think about football with the widest possible lens, and they will provide a complementary depth of economic, sociological and political guidance.

Since the founding of the first North American Soccer League (NASL) in 1968, no outdoor football league, men or women, has ever generated a profit.

Research shows that this half-century of losses year-in year-out, is due to three factors:

First, the branding strategy that football has adopted,

Second, the misapplication of the proper business model at the league and club level, and

Third, the motivation (or a lack thereof) to adopt the global standard of excellence at the football league and club level.

To maximize the full potential of football across the entire football pyramid (from youth to the professional ranks) we must strive to be the best in a global context.

We will argue that an internal conflict or even what can be called a war is being waged across various levels of the USA's football pyramid – this war is a war of excellence versus mediocrity.

Chapter 1 begins with a discussion about branding, because in all of the literature and commentary about what is wrong with football in the USA, very little or no substantive critique of branding has been made.

Chapter 2 is a discussion of comparative football league and club benchmarks, namely, the global standard of football excellence; the five (5) revenue drivers of football clubs; fan membership/ownership of football clubs; and lastly, the five (5) football club business models.

Chapter 3 provides reference materials that provide a political and sociological frame of reference. Given the structure of team sports' ownership in the United States, we find that sport replicates the overall structure of society. Only the wealthy are capable of owning sports teams and the product they sell is sold to the general public as any other commodity.

Our purpose is to counter-balance that position and establish fan and community membership/ownership of football clubs as a new paradigm.

This idea carries significant political and sociological impacts – impacts which all football fans should be prepared to understand and deal with. The reference materials in Chapter 3 are there to help prepare you for the ideological challenges that the proposals being made here will engender.

CHAPTER 1: THE FOOTBALL MANIFESTO OR WHY REBRANDING FOOTBALL IS IMPORTANT

"Habermas describes an ideal speech situation, an interaction in which each party has an equal chance to speak unencumbered by authority and in which norms of comprehensibility, sincerity, legitimacy, and truthfulness are upheld, as the standard by which to critique ideological domination. Marketing is a form of distorted communication in that marketers control the information that is exchanged. Marketers organize the code, and we as consumers have no choice but to participate."
--- Douglas B. Holt, Why Do Brands Cause Trouble?

"The triumph of advertising in the culture industry is that consumers feel compelled to buy and use its products even though they see through them."
--- Theodore W. Adorno, Dialectic of Enlightenment: Philosophical Fragments

The research behind this book began immediately after the 2014 World Cup in Brazil. During those games three statistics about USA fan support caught my attention.

First, the USA represented the largest fan contingent that visited Brazil for WC14.

Second, during the tournament Facebook and Twitter both broke usage records.

Third, the USA-Portugal match was the most watched football match in the history of the United States, exceeding the ratings that year of the National Basketball Association (NBA) finals, Major League Baseball (MLB)'s World Series and the National Hockey League (NHL)'s finals.

To set the record straight, the most watched football match in the USA to date now applies to the 2015 Women's World Cup Final, which saw the USWNT beat Japan.

All of this begs a question. If the demand for world-class football in the USA exists, why isn't the USA world-class on the field and off?

During the research for this book, this question was juxtaposed against the success of the Big 4.

If each of the Big 4 leagues represents the global standard of excellence in their respective sport, why after 20+ years is Major League Soccer (MLS) not even close to being the global standard of excellence for football?

One of the key reasons is branding.

For nearly 50 years, professional football has consistently adopted the Big 4's generic branding strategy for its leagues and teams, meaning that it has always attempted to acquire market share in an already saturated market place for that particular branding strategy. When taking into consideration that the Big 4 generate approximately 25 billion a year in revenue, there is simply no room left for that particular branding and marketing strategy.

Football needs to be rebranded. But before we deal with that crucial issue, another important distinction needs to be made – the difference between a soccer team and a football club.

1.1 Soccer Teams v. Football Clubs

Any analysis of football in the USA would be remiss if it did not begin by drawing an important distinction between a soccer team and a football club. This is the first conceptual step in rebranding football.

The USA's professional sports teams (i.e., the Big 4) are owned by one wealthy individual or groups of wealthy individuals.

In continental Europe and Latin America one of the key differentiating factors of the sport of football is the concept of the football club. This distinction between team and club is at the core essence of football culture.

Flamengo is a membership club based in the Gàvea neighborhood of Rio de Janeiro. As mentioned, Flamengo began as a rowing club at the end of the 19th century, but soon evolved to include football. What most people outside of Brazil and Latin America do not know is that Flamengo fields teams in basketball, volleyball, tennis, handball, futsal, swimming, judo, jiu-jitsu, gymnastics and a number of other sports, which are part of what every member gets for his/her monthly fee. Think of Flamengo as a branded version of the YWCA or the YMCA. Most of the major Olympic sports can be found at Flamengo. And for a monthly fee anyone can join. Needless to say a full-array of weight-training and aerobic facilities are available daily to members.

Boca Juniors in Buenos Aires operates under the same format, as do most of the major clubs in South America. Real Madrid and Barcelona operate under a similar model.

It is this football club concept that serves as a key component and foundation for football culture.

The club's venue (stadium and training facilities), colors, club songs, club support groups, the merchandising and licensing of the different club sports, the club sponsors (some of whom may in fact be wealthy individuals), along with a variety of corporate/commercial sponsors and TV/digital sponsors make up a significant portion of the revenue streams that maintain the club in operational equilibrium day-in day-out.

Football clubs are a 24/7 community resource. Literally, tens of thousands of people in Brazil, Argentina and other countries in the region hold memberships in such clubs. The same is true in continental Europe, particularly in Germany where club membership/ownership is mandated by law (the U.K. is a major exception to this rule albeit they do have a supporter's trust movement).

In the United States you can spend USD 150 million on a franchise fee, another USD 150 million or more on a stadium, stick a brand on it, and think that you are riding high in the world of football. Nothing could be further from the truth.

Without this concept of a football club, a true football culture in the USA and Canada will never be established.

Establishing football clubs in the USA and Canada is the key to the future.

We will explore the football club in more detail when we discuss the five (5) football club business models below.

1.2 THE FOOTBALL MANIFESTO

No existing or predecessor professional league has been able to crack the conundrum of unlocking football's full revenue generating potential in the United States and Canada.

The current set of soccer team brands, and all predecessor brands across all prior professional league attempts since 1968, both men and women, guarantee that the full upside potential, both financially and in terms of the sport's cultural and media impact locally, nationally and globally, will not be maximized.

Rather than unlocking football's potential, these league and team names simply maintain the status quo of an underperforming and undervalued live entertainment product.

Soccer, as soccer, is part of the sport's value "lock down" at the youth, amateur and professional level.

The word soccer has had negative psychological impacts across all levels of society for decades, and in and of itself, carries a stigma and a hidden meaning – that as a sport it is not worthy of the name football.

Professional soccer carries an inherent notion of second-class citizenship in the world of sports in the United States and Canada.

The sport's rightful name, the name that fully and logically applies to what this sport is all about, the name that resonates with what the mind actually sees, is the key first step to rebranding the sport and realizing professional football's full value.

The refusal to call this sport what it is, to be intimidated by third parties in the use of terminology that accurately describes what the product is, to remain unconscious about the process of manufactured consent and indoctrination, interferes with a deeper connection to the sport and undermines monetization.

In essence, soccer is the sport's slave name.

True liberation requires an assumption, or better a reclaiming of the sport's rightful mantle as football.

Football is the sport's birthright.

It therefore stands to reason that the current set of brands and all brands from the past, were born amidst an unconscious mindset of inferiority. In this light, football is a rectification.

It is a bringing to consciousness of what was previously masked and erroneously assumed to be a natural state of affairs.

Soccer is not a natural state of affairs. Football is.

If we begin with the fundamental premise that we want to create the best professional football league in the world in the United States and Canada, and simultaneously maximize monetization, return on investment and fan and community ownership and impact, we have to face a fundamental truth -- this will only occur with (i) a top-to-bottom re-branding of the sport, (ii) a restructuring of the business model from youth football to the professional ranks, and (iii) the adoption and full application of the global standards of excellence for leagues and clubs.

The value driver is re-branding.

Rebranding is the catalyst for change and sets the stage for a different professional football league and club business model.

To summarize, to achieve the goal of the USA becoming #1 in the world of football requires:

(1) a restructuring of the entire football pyramid, not simply the professional leagues,

(2) a willingness to experiment with rebranding strategies and alternative business models that have been de-risked and proven elsewhere, and

(3) a marrying of these efforts with bold experimentation in new technology and non-technology strategies that impact the entire football pyramid, from youth to the pros.

1.3 Why is Rebranding Important?

Rebranding is important because it creates a new foundation for (i) fan and community owned football clubs, (ii) monetization and (iii) the creation of a true football culture.

1.4 The Current Branding Paradigm

We know these brands. They are household names. The Cowboys, the Yankees, the Giants, the Red Wings, the Red Sox, the Knicks, the Lakers, the Blackhawks, the Heat, etc.

When we look at the names of the teams in Major League Soccer (MLS), the National Women's Soccer League (NWSL), the United Soccer League (USL) and the North American Soccer League (NASL), we find that the majority of brands are cut from the same cloth.

Some MLS teams like D.C. United, Minnesota United, Real Salt Lake or Orlando City, have attempted to bring the spirit of European clubs to the United States by using *United* or *Real* or *City,* in their names.

The most recent trend is to append FC to a city as in NYCFC, Atlanta FC, FC Cincinnati and in Los Angeles, LAFC.

The point is that these brands fail to sufficiently differentiate professional football from the Big 4. Their chance of breaking into an already saturated marketplace is slim. But this must be said with a few qualifications to provide a larger context.

The first response to the allegation that these new brands are not working, will be those who point to both MLS's Seattle Sounders and the Atlanta FC franchises and say, how do you explain respectively 42,000 and

46,000 on average game day attendance and then state that the brand is not working?

Here is the counter-argument.

1.5 Three (3) Tiers of Football Club Brands

Three of the five revenue drivers of football are crucial: venues, TV and commercial.

MLS is structured to rely on game day gate receipts as the principal driver of revenue (one aspect of venues). The other revenue drivers are dramatically below the global benchmarks of first division leagues and clubs in Europe.

The fact that Seattle and Atlanta are driving that much traffic to their stadia on game day is a major accomplishment (although I would like to see how many free complementary tickets compose the average gate, not just for Seattle and Atlanta, but for the entire league), but it is not nearly enough to grant world-class status to either club, the league or the respective cities.

More importantly for our rebranding discussion, the demographic trends of the last 25 years in the USA and Canada have created a deep and varied cultural mosaic. The new influx of ethnicity, language, culture and history has created a deep pool from which to draw cultural inspiration for new unprecedented football club brands.

Football club brands can be divided into three (3) tiers.

A **Tier 1 Brand** would be a global football club brand that has strong domestic <u>and</u> international appeal. The best analogies would be Manchester United, Real Madrid, Barcelona or Bayern Münich.

A **Tier 2 Brand** would be a football club brand that is nationally recognized, revered and sought after – a brand having commercial impact and monetization potential demonstrated across the entire USA and Canada.

A **Tier 3 Brand** is a local or regional brand that resonates in that given geography and within that geography maintains a dominant commercial and community presence.

Seattle and Atlanta both represent solid Tier 3 Brands. They carry weight locally. Across the professional football leagues in the USA and Canada we can find several legitimate Tier 3 Brands.

A true football club brand becomes distinguished from a just another team name, by becoming a sustainable value creation mechanism that drives and grows monetization over time.

Brands must work hand-in-hand with football club and league business models to maximize value. Either one alone is not enough.

The current team names do not drive sustainable value creation and monetization across all five revenue drivers, and therefore, do not rise to the level of becoming true brands.

1.6 Why and How Brands Matter

There are a number of teams that derive their names from the original North American Soccer League (NASL), which was at its height in the mid to late 1970s.

In the minds of most league officials, current investors and team owners, there is some, but at bottom, little connection between team names, revenue generation, value creation and return on investment. The real driver of value creation in their minds is the sport itself.

The brand, therefore, enhances the value, but it doesn't drive the value.

In this context, the argument goes that practically *any name* will do.

On the face of it, this rings true. But reality tells a different story about how to create value.

To an extent there is a clear recognition by some investors about the need for rebranding.

What has been less understood is how to link a new brand to sustainable monetization on the level of our global benchmarks for football club branding, FC Barcelona, FC Bayern München and Manchester United, etc.

For instance, in addition to the old NASL names being used in professional football leagues today (i.e., Timbers, Sounders, Whitecaps, Cosmos, Dynamo, Rowdies, etc.), there has been an attempt (referenced above) to Europeanize or Latinize football branding, but this has met with only marginal success.

Sporting Kansas City, D.C. *United*, *Real* Salt Lake, the old Chivas USA and the New York Cosmos, are all examples of a straightforward importing of a brand (or an aspect of a brand) and simply attaching it to a city, geographic region or demographic.

The problem with this approach is that it remains a "surface based market analysis of branding." The thought process and analysis of brand development is too shallow and fails to penetrate at a demographic depth that triggers sustainable and improving monetization.

1.7 The Case of Sporting Kansas City

Is Sporting Kansas City a better brand than the prior name of the Wizards or the Wiz? Probably, but that is not the question. The question is what connects and monetizes at or near (or possibly even exceeds) the football club benchmarks of FC Barcelona, FC Bayern Münich and Manchester United?

Let's put this analysis in context. The three European brands mentioned are Tier 1 brands. Tier 1 brands generate a global fan following. Tier 2 brands generate a national following, and Tier 3 brands generate a strictly local or regional following.

It could be argued, therefore, that in comparing Sporting Kansas City to FC Barcelona we are arguing apples and oranges. We are comparing a clearly local brand in Sporting Kansas City with a global brand in FC Barcelona.

In the same way that the United States and Canada have 123 professional sports teams across the Big 4, Europe too has hundreds of football clubs, some which have used United, Real and Sporting in their names for over a century.

In both the case of the United States and Canada, and Europe, those brands have saturated their respective markets and in some truly rare cases like FC Barcelona, FC Bayern Münich and Manchester United, they have not only become dominant in their home markets, they have become major global brands, that monetize globally.

Finding the right brand sets off a sustainable chain reaction of carving out a unique and sustainable share of the Kansas City metropolitan area marketplace for pro sports. Maximizing the monetary impact of that carve out can only occur with deep and broad demographic research – research that goes far deeper into the collective psyche of the region than has occurred with any other professional team sport.

Such a process is not simply about importing ideas from another country, continent or culture from Europe or Latin America, or about borrowing ideas from the dominant professional sports culture of the United States.

It is about discovering something new. The first order of business is to find a new brand that will dominate the Tier 3 space and rival the best team sport's brands in that metropolitan area, on a dollar for dollar basis.

The second order of business is to link that new brand to a new business and football club ownership model that treats the fans as partners, owners and value added contributors in a new community based democratic process of club administration.

In Sporting Kansas City's case, the pre-fix *Sporting*, has absolutely nothing to do with Kansas City, its history, culture and demographics. The team could have been rebranded as Kansas City *United* or *Real* Kansas City and had the same or near similar effect and impact.

In point of fact, the real attractor and value proposition in Kansas City is three-fold: (i) the existing grassroots demand for the sport (with the Kansas City region being one of the strongest youth football areas in the country), (ii) a market that is not saturated with pro sports (i.e., the NFL Chiefs and MLB's Royals), and (iii) what is arguably the most technologically advanced stadium for football in the United States.

One might argue that brands take decades to establish, but this is simply not true.

Even a sense of tradition can be manufactured with the right brand. What took decades in the past can now be digitally launched in a matter of weeks or months, and have measurable and even dramatic impact in a year or even less.

Digital changes everything. We live in a global economy, where the planet is increasingly becoming an omni-channel e-commerce driven digital platform, accessible via broadband and mobile devices.

In saturated professional sports marketplaces like the United States, Canada, and Europe, we have to remember that our minds and particularly the minds of youth (a key and possibly *the key demographic* for professional football) are absorbing the professional football product and the advertising surrounding the sport, irrespective of borders and increasingly irrespective of language barriers.

The conclusion is that a stronger brand exists and has yet to be uncovered in the Kansas City metropolitan area.

The same arguments made with respect to Sporting Kansas City, that stronger more monetizable brands exist, can be applied to D.C. United and Real Salt Lake. We can extend the analysis further to the San Jose Earthquakes, the Chicago Fire, the Colorado Rapids, the Crew, the New England Revolution, the Los Angeles Galaxy, the Montreal Manic, NYCFC, and the list goes on. Nor is this analysis limited to MLS. It applies to all of the professional football leagues in the United States and Canada.

Practically, without exception all of these teams could benefit from rebranding -- and benefit doubly with an adjustment in their business and ownership models.

For those who feel that Seattle, Portland, Orlando and Atlanta are exceptions that need no rebranding, I would tend to agree, with the caveat that an adjustment in the business and ownership structure cannot be avoided, if world-class status is the goal.

In the case of Chivas USA, however, we have a different analysis to employ.

1.8 The Case of Chivas USA

Chivas USA is an important case because it is centered in the global mega-city of Los Angeles.

Well over a decade ago when Chivas USA was founded, the basic premise was to use a well-known and dominant football club brand from the top-tier of Mexican football in Los Angeles.

Given that Los Angeles has a significant Mexican presence (i.e., Mexicans represent 50% of Los Angeles County's population of 10 million), the name Club Deportivo (C.D.) Guadalajara was already well known.

C.D. Guadalajara (or Chivas the club's nickname) is one of the most popular teams in Mexico.

Guadalajara plays in the Liga MX and has 11 First Division titles, 7 Campeón de Campeones, 1 InterLiga, 1 Copa Challenger, 4 Copa Oros de Occidente and 2 Copa México trophies.

Guadalajara is one of the ten founding members of the Mexican First Division and with longstanding rivals Club América has never been relegated to the Second Division. The club took second place in the famed Copa Libertadores in 2010. Founded in 1906, Guadalajara is without question one of the truly great football clubs in the Americas.

Chivas USA, however, was viewed as the "little brother" or worse, as Guadalajara's B team for Los Angeles.

For ten years Chivas USA never got traction on the field or off, and in February 2014, MLS "bought back" Chivas USA from its owners (who still own C.D. Guadalajara).

The new ownership group for the rebranded Chivas franchise, LAFC, is led by Peter Guber and Henry Nyugen.

Before examining their exercise in rebranding an MLS franchise in LA, we need to ask what are the lessons learned from Chivas USA?

The first lesson, is that importing an established football brand does not work.

If importing parts of brands like *Sporting*, *United* and *Real* doesn't work (when compared against our global benchmarks), we now have confirmation that importing the entire brand is a fiasco, even if that brand is a major success in its home country. Why?

Because the Mexicans in Los Angeles are knowledgeable football fans. They have a deeply embedded global standard of excellence.

Even if there were Guadalajara fans living Los Angeles, no die-hard seasoned football fan wants to spend their hard earned cash on a B team. Or for what is at best, from their perspective, a second division league in MLS.

That is why true football fans across the United States, turn out to see the real thing – friendlies involving Manchester United, FC Barcelona, Real Madrid, Chelsea, etc.

The second lesson is that if these same European football powerhouses used their global brands to establish a club "for the United States and Canada" they would fail for the same reasons that Chivas USA failed – they are not the "real thing," and they represent a product below the globally accepted standard of excellence.

It would appear to stand to reason then, that the issue is simply the quality of the product on the field, and that the football club brand is at best of secondary importance.

If world-class talent could be imported, so the argument goes, then the fans will turn out, irrespective of the brand.

The devil's advocate for this position would say look at the old Cosmos with Pelé, Beckenbauer, Carlos Alberto, etc.

Which brings us to a third lesson, namely that the idea of importing aging talent was not the solution or a sustainable investment strategy for the first incarnation of the Cosmos or the NASL (or the second incarnation of either), much less Chivas USA.

MLS has its own version of the "importing talent" idea in the Beckham Rule, which experienced an adjustment in 2012, to accommodate younger players as well.

Even so, the Beckham Rule, coupled with MLS's salary cap restrictions, and little priority on the five revenue drivers of professional football, has produced after 20+ years, a product on the field and off, that is considerably below the standards of excellence maintained by the global benchmarks of the EPL and Bundesliga for leagues and clubs.

Clearly, there is demand for professional football in the United States and Canada.

Importantly, however, that demand is being driven by strong demographic trends in both countries that carry long-term implications for the sport.

New immigrants and existing ethnic groups with a strong cultural connection to the sport are driving football into the mainstream and down into the grassroots. They will not compromise their global standards of excellence.

1.9 The Case of LAFC

Los Angeles is the second largest Spanish speaking city on the planet (behind Mexico City). This south-of-the-border cultural influence has become so strong, that U.S. Soccer is now avoiding USA v. Mexican national team games in Los Angeles, because the huge crowds are overwhelmingly supporting the Mexican national team at the expense of the USMNT.

There are some great football cities around the world: London, Barcelona, Madrid, Buenos Aires, São Paulo and Rio de Janeiro are among them. Based on demographics, Los Angeles is a prime candidate to become a world-class football city.

At this point, it simply lacks the world-class football club(s) that it deserves. LAFC gives no indication that it will be that football club for several reasons.

First, LAFC has built its own 22,000 seat stadium (Banc of California Stadium) in the Exposition Park neighborhood of Los Angeles. 22,000 seats by definition ends all discussion regarding the ability of a club to become world-class.

We will discuss stadium size at some length below, but suffice it say that 22,000 seats is below the average of the British and German second divisions.

Second, MLS has already proven that given its branding and business strategy, it is hard pressed to find support for two teams in Los Angeles.

Third, the LA Galaxy is being touted as LAFC's cross-town rival, but that is based on location alone. There is nothing that is culturally-driven and sustainable setting up that rivalry, any more than the (non-) rivalry between the Galaxy and Chivas, and they both played in the Galaxy stadium (27,000) for a decade (a similar concocted rivalry exists with the New York Red Bulls and NYCFC – both examples are the soccer equivalent (not the football equivalent) of dueling McDonald's franchises).

The distinguishing characteristics about LAFC are the brand, the local ownership group and the fact that the team will play in its own football stadium.

There may be an argument that says that Peter Guber will be able to guarantee the glitz of Hollywood attendees at games and in a 22,000 seater how hard could it be to fill it?

Strangely enough, the Hollywood crowd loves a winner (think the Lakers) but it also respects and only supports on-the-field/court excellence. LAFC categorically will not have that.

Time will tell, but the LAFC product in my mind does not have the requisite pieces of the puzzle that Los Angeles deserves. The MLS business model destroys any hope of that occurring.

The key last point is this: LAFC, as a brand, shows that no creative in-depth homework was done on the cultural milieu of Los Angeles as one of the world's great melting pots.

No thought was given to passion and how to best connect people through their culture, their history, events and/or personalities (these are just some of the components of a culture to consider for football club branding purposes).

Of course the brand guru's that came up with LAFC will say that they did just that. They will argue that they wanted to bring everyone together and that LAFC stands for that (instead of basing a new brand on one particular ethnic group for instance).

Lamentably, LAFC is simply an attempt to attract everyone in the LA metro area to the sport and not the brand.

The message from MLS is clear – just slap FC behind any city name and you have your brand.

Los Angeles deserves to have its own version of Barcelona, Real Madrid or Manchester United.

However, given that LA is now home to two NFL franchises, the likelihood of MLS being able to carve out a piece of the market beyond the size of the market that the Galaxy has achieved is remote at best.

The glitz that Peter Guber can muster won't be able to overcome the Tier 3 brand status of LAFC. They may sell-out every game, but LAFC won't be the world-class football club that LA deserves.

The challenge for Los Angeles football fans is to create a football club brand not simply to rival the fan support networks of the Lakers, the Clippers, the Rams, the Chargers, the Kings, the Mighty Ducks, the Dodgers, the Angels, etc.

The challenge is to create a football club brand in LA that rivals Manchester United, Barcelona and Real Madrid.

One analogy that comes to mind from a branding perspective is São Paulo FC (founded in 1930) from the city of São Paulo in Brazil. São Paulo is one of the world's largest cities at more than 21 million people. São Paulo FC is one of Brazil's great football club brands, but the club plays in a city where it goes up against other huge global brands like Corinthians, Palmeiras and Santos.

São Paulo F.C. plays in Pacaembu stadium (capacity: 40,199). Corinthians plays in Corinthians Arena (capacity: 49,205). Palmeiras FC plays in Allianz Parque (capacity: 43,713) and Santos FC plays in Estadio Vila Belmiro (capacity: 16,798).

16,798? Santos' stadium, like most of the older facilities, is now an all-seater, but prior to that, during Pelé's years for example, the entire stadium was an open grandstand with no designated seating and a standing section. That old model routinely held more than 30,000.

One response to the São Paulo FC idea is that the club was founded in 1930 and all LAFC needs is time. To reiterate, given the digital world we live in, a killer brand gets traction rapidly. LAFC may outdraw the Galaxy. My point is that if that proves to be the case, at 22,000 you haven't accomplished much. If you cannot draw 50-60,000 fans or more per game in Los Angeles there is something wrong.

The USA and Canada together have the largest football support network outside of Western Europe.

These supporters do not spend their money on the Big 4. They are not Big 4 season ticket holders. They do not attend Big 4 games. They represent an untapped non-monetized consumer support network of immense proportions.

Los Angeles' fan base for world-class football is one of the best in the world.

LAFC's fate will depend on the evolution of football in Los Angeles and generally in the USA.

LA, Chicago and New York City are the obvious candidates for billion dollar plus football club franchise values.

Our argument here is that that value creation for a billion dollar football club ideally begins with a Tier 1 brand, not a Tier 3 brand.

1.10 What Would a Billion Dollar Football Club Brand Look Like?

Let's take the New York City metropolitan area as an example. A billion dollar brand will link the existing suburban football support network with urban New York City-based ethnic groups (mostly from Europe, the Caribbean and Latin America) with an established history and cultural understanding of the sport.

The new brand will connect with the community more deeply than any existing or past football club brand.

At this new level of psychic connection is a depth of passion and commitment that has no precedent in the United States and Canada, and it is at this visceral and tribal inner core that a dedicated consumer-owner and life-time football supporter is found.

The United States is the only country in the world today where re-branding can create billion dollar football brands in three to five years.

Nor is this phenomenon limited in its potential to New York City. The digitally driven social media world, allows for brand creation and impact on a global scale, in ever-shorter periods of time.

This means that new brands can be created that match and even exceed the global brand appeal of Manchester United, Barcelona, Real Madrid and other leading football brands.

The question is -- what is the secret sauce? How do you unearth, create and launch that kind of a brand?

Football is a global product that fits squarely within Steve Stoute's idea of tanning, as referred to and described in his book and the VH-1 video series *The Tanning of America*.

1.11 The Power of Tanning

Tanning is a phenomenon that reflects the melding together of racial, religious and cultural backgrounds, often with a youth-focused undercurrent of urban, hip-hop and cultural creatives across a digitized network of global villages.

It is a process of inclusion not exclusion. It is also a reflection of a deep tribal connection across our species.

Tanning manifests itself in music, the arts, in design, in food, in all aspects of business, and potentially on and off the football field as well.

Lastly, *tanning* has to do with *interior mental landscapes*. We can all be tan.

No two countries are better positioned to exploit the *tanning* of football globally, than the United States and Canada.

The next great harvest of football brands that have global impact will be created in the United States and Canada.

Some of these new brands will draw and monetize from a local or regional fan base, or even a national one, but the best of these new brands will monetize via a global fan base.

Think of New York City, Los Angeles, Chicago, Toronto and other melting pot cities where cross-cultural and cross-generational melding is the norm. These metropolitan areas will produce some of the great Tier 1 and Tier 2 brands in this new vision for professional football.

The process of discovering these new brands requires an unprecedented plunge into the collective psychic, cultural and historical depths of the United States' and Canada's evolving demographics. It is there that we find the essence of football's *tanning and branding potential*.

The argument for rebranding football is based on one simple fact. Football is more than a sport -- it is a culture.

Rebranding is a realization that there is another deeper level of cultural connectedness, which has no precedent in the world of professional sports in the United States and Canada.

This deeper level unites us, triggers our collective passions and importantly has not been fully tapped into in terms of its commercial potential.

CHAPTER 2: THE GLOBAL STANDARD OF EXCELLENCE, THE FIVE (5) REVENUE DRIVERS OF FOOTBALL, FAN MEMBERSHIP/OWNERSHIP OF FOOTBALL CLUBS AND THE FIVE (5) CLUB BUSINESS MODELS

"All that I know about morality and obligations I owe to football."
--- Albert Camus
"In a football match everything is complicated by the presence of the other team."
--- Jean-Paul Sartre
"I don't believe skill was, or ever will be, the result of coaches. It is a result of a love affair between the child and the ball."
--- Roy Maurice Keene, former captain of Ireland and Manchester United

2.1 The Global Standard of Excellence

The global standard of excellence for football leagues, and here we make one of our key assumptions, is best represented by the English Premier League (EPL) and the German Bundesliga.

Whereas the global standard of excellence for football clubs includes Manchester United, Manchester City,

Chelsea, Arsenal, Tottenham, Bayern Münich, Borussia Dortmund, Schalke 04, Real Madrid, Barcelona, Juventus, Milan, PSG, etc.

Both standards of excellence are European. This does not mean that important lessons can't be found in Latin America, and where applicable we will point those out.

How do we achieve the global standard of excellence at the league and club level?

Part of the answer is rebranding football. The other part of the answer is a differentiated focus on revenue and on proven alternative football club business models.

2.2   The Five (5) Revenue Drivers of Professional Football Clubs

The five revenue drivers of football result from the maturity of the football product as a whole. Europe is the best example of that.

In the United States only the first three drivers are relevant and within the context of professional football (i.e., MLS) only attendance, an aspect of the first, venues, is the principal operational driver of revenue.

The five (5) revenue drivers of football clubs are:

Venues – which includes stadia, capacity issues, club and training facilities, club membership, ticket pricing, parking, concessions, and all revenues that are generated via the physical infrastructure that supports the sport – most of which are generated on the day of the match – hence **Match Day Revenue.**

On-Field Product Distribution – which includes all aspects of TV, media and digital exploitation, generically – **TV Revenue.**

Off-Field Product Distribution – which includes brand development, merchandising & licensing (including e-commerce) and corporate sponsorships, otherwise known as – **Commercial Revenue**

Managing Talent – which includes players, managers and officials, and

Packaging Productions – which includes league and club competitions, both domestic and international

You should memorize these. These 5 factors should be on the tip of your tongue in any discussion about the future of football in the USA (or anywhere).

2.3 Fan Membership/Ownership of Football Clubs and the Five (5) Football Club Business Models

Club Model #1: The Barcelona Model.

Real Madrid and Barcelona are 100% owned and controlled by their fans. Real Madrid has 91,000 dues paying members. Barcelona has over 180,000 dues paying members. All of these members have a vote. Both clubs operate as not-for-profit corporations (NFPs), but are ranked nevertheless as two of the most valuable football clubs on the planet. [1]

Forbes values Barcelona (in 2017) at USD 3.64 billion and Real Madrid at USD 3.58 billion, making them #2 and #3 worldwide in terms of football club valuations.

Football clubs that are 100% owned by the fans will be called the Barcelona Model.

Club Model #2: The Bayern Münich Model

While the EPL is one of the best examples of maximizing revenue (it is the #1 football league in the world in that category) it is one of the worst examples of fan membership/ownership of football clubs.

The best example of fan ownership of football clubs goes to Germany. Germany also has the highest average attendance of any football league in the world at roughly 42,000 per game.

Germany has passed legislation at the federal level (meaning countrywide application) requiring the 50% + 1 share rule. This means that the fans in the Bundesliga must have 50% + 1 share (meaning voting control) of any and all teams in the league (the prime examples being football clubs in the first and second divisions of the Bundesliga).

The three exceptions to fan membership/ownership control in the first division of the Bundesliga are Bayern 04 Leverkusen (owned by Bayer, the pharmaceutical company) and VfL Wolfsburg (owned by Volkswagen) – both of these teams were grandfathered in and otherwise adhere to the administrative parameters of the Bundesliga. RB Leipzig (owned by Red Bull) is another corporate exception. [2]

One of Germany's best examples of the fan ownership model at work is Bayern München.

All football clubs in Germany are structured (again by law) in the following way: the equivalent of a USA not-for-profit corporation (NFP or in German e.V.) owns and operates the club and admits club members, whose dues in part support the club (along with the other 5 drivers of revenue).

Clubs are largely focused on football, but may also embrace and support other sports. All sports are considered amateur or youth focused and considered to be community resources and therefore fall under the umbrella of the NFP (e.V.). Normally the only exception is club involvement with professional football.

Professional football is usually structured in a separate legal vehicle, or what we would call in the USA a limited liability company or LLC (in Germany it is called GmbH). And here is where the 50% + 1 share rule applies. The NFP (e.V.) club must own at least 50% +1 share of the LLC (GmbH).

In Bayern Münich's case the NFP (e.V.) club owns 75% of the LLC (GmbH)(or 75% of the team that we see on TV), while 25% is equally split between three corporations, Adidas, Audi and Alliance Insurance (each with 8.33%). The NFP (e.V.) hires a professional management team to administer the LLC (GmbH) and its professional football business on a day-to-day basis.

Youth teams below in the NFP (e.V.) serve as feeder mechanisms for the professional ranks.

It is important to recognize that the German model emphasizes club membership (as opposed to ownership). Shares generally are not negotiable. This means that in the vast majority of cases, clubs cannot be bought and sold. Clubs are viewed as a permanent community resource (historically there have been exceptions to this rule, but the exceptions are few).

We will call fan owned teams via the 50% + 1 Rule, the Bundesliga or Bayern Münich Model.

Therefore, there are two fan owned football club models where the fans have control of the club – the Barcelona Model (100% fan owned) and the Bayern Münich Model (at least 50% + 1 share of fan ownership).

What follows is a discussion where fans maintain (i) a minority position in the ownership structure of the club or (ii) where fans have absolutely no stake in the ownership and management of the club.

Club Model #3: The Swansea City Model

Manchester United is owned by the Glazer family (owner of the Tampa Bay Bucaneers of the NFL) and is publicly traded on the New York Stock Exchange (NYSE). Forbes ranks Manchester United at #1 with a value of USD 3.69 billion.

The fans who own shares of Man U via the NYSE do not have voting power. In essence, they have purchased shares out of a love for the club, in very much the same way that fans of the Green Bay Packers have acquired "vanity" shares. These fans have no voting power and no voice in the management of the club they support.

A better example of fans maintaining a minority stake and having a voice in a club's business affairs is Swansea City AFC of the EPL.

Majority control shareholders Stephen Kaplan and Jason Levien hold 68% of the voting shares, while Swansea City Supporters Society Ltd (a fan support group) owns 21.1% of the voting shares and maintains a seat on the club's board of directors.

We call this the Swansea City Model

Club Model #4: The Chelsea Model

Chelsea FC is owned by Roman Abramovich. This ownership model where one extremely wealthy individual (or a group of wealthy individuals) owns 100% voting control of the club, we will call the Chelsea Model.

The Chelsea Model is the standard ownership model of the Big 4 professional sports teams in the USA. Fans under this model are simply and only consumers. They have no ownership and no say in the management of the club. Under this model an owner may decide to move his club to another city and the fans can do nothing about it.

Club Model #5: The MLS Model

At the far extreme of wealthy individual owners of football clubs is Major League Soccer (MLS).

Under the MLS ownership structure investors are known as investor-operators. All investors invest in MLS itself, a Delaware LLC. In exchange each investor-operator secures the right to operate a franchise in a given geographic area.

This is a departure from the traditional ownership model of the Big 4 and we will discuss its implications below when we explore the details of the MLS business model. We will call this approach the MLS Model.

The Football Manifesto is about the future, but it is also about correcting the mistakes made in the past.

Despite the criticism being leveled at U.S. Soccer-MLS/SUM, both in the United States generally amongst the rank and file supporters of football, and even with this book, we have to acknowledge what has been accomplished by U.S. Soccer-MLS/SUM, despite the disturbing conclusions which will be explored in depth in the following pages.

That said, and given the realities of business, the most likely outcome for the future of the sport in the United States (and Canada), is a mix of business models for professional football clubs.

Today, the overwhelmingly dominant model in the USA is the MLS Model (which will be dealt with in Chapter 5: Major League Soccer (MLS): The Lid on the Pressure Cooker of Demand for Football).

The three models which carry the potential to transform the United States into a global football power are the Barcelona Model, the Bayern Münich Model and the Swansea City Model.

The Football Manifesto will be launching a new league and new football clubs that embody these three football club business models and the branding strategy described and embodied herein, as part of its second edition.

Obviously, this new approach to creating a true football culture in the United States, will have to take into consideration how we migrate from the dysfunctionality we currently have to the status of being #1 in the world. Therefore, accommodations and plans for the migration of the existing paradigm to a new paradigm will be an integral part of the second edition of The Football Manifesto.

[1] While the number of dues paying club members of Real Madrid and Barcelona is impressive, the evolution of those clubs has created mechanisms in each club that steers the election of top administrative officials towards small cohesive groups that largely dominate election results.

[2] RB Leipzig took a different route to the first division. The club was founded in 2009 by the Red Bull company, which bought a fifth division team called SSV Markranstädt and renamed it. Their plan was to take eight years to arrive at the first division, which they accomplished. Needless to say, this is a strategy that needs further exploration and understanding.

CHAPTER 3: UNDERSTANDING FOOTBALL FROM AN IDEOLOGICAL PERSPECTIVE

"Democracy is two wolves and a lamb voting on what to have for lunch.   Liberty is a well-armed lamb contesting the vote."
--- Anon

Every chapter in this book will hopefully be educative. This means bringing you information you did not know before or providing a new insightful angle on what you did know.

Education continually forces the mind to open and that is both its strength and the nature of the threat it represents.

The more people know the more difficult they are to control and have them do an authority figure's or a dictator's bidding.   People who think for themselves represent a societal wild-card for others who thrive on centralizing control.   Education, is therefore, by its very nature, subversive from the perspective of those in power.

Democracy in the United States has been subverted. Not surprisingly, the democratic processes that govern football have been subverted as well.   Weighted voting at U.S. Soccer is not an accident.

The idea of empowering fans with the tools to take football into their own hands will be viewed by many as subversive.

When anyone or any group challenges the business status quo or challenges entrenched and powerful monopoly interests (irrespective of the industry vertical) they are traditionally labeled as anti-establishment or worse as radical, socialist or communist.

This labeling, however, only occurs when "outsiders" participate in such efforts.

3.1 Working Within the System

For instance, in the USA in the 1980s a wave of corporate take-overs occurred, whereby financial institutions (i.e., banks and investment banks) lent substantial amounts of capital (usually in the billions of dollars) to finance the take-over by a small group of investors (i.e., private equity professionals – the providers of equity capital as opposed to debt) of a targeted "underperforming" company.

These so-called corporate raiders usually attended the best academic institutions (i.e., the Ivy League) and worked post-graduation at many of the elite investment firms on Wall Street (e.g., Goldman Sachs, etc.) before venturing into the marketplace as independent value creation experts and opportunists.

Companies that became/become takeover targets in most cases were/are demonstrably underperforming to such an extent, that a proposed change of management and a reorientation of the business model by the private equity investors gives clear indications that as a revamped company, the new cash flow profile would be sufficient to pay off the debt (loans) from the financing institutions and provide a solid return on investment (usually a multiple of the equity investment made by the PE team).

A book, *Barbarians at the Gate*, tells an interesting story of the takeover of Nabisco by the buy-out firm KKR, which when it occurred in the late 1980s was the largest buy-out in history. Was KKR considered anti-establishment, radical, socialist or communist? No. Not by any stretch of the imagination. Some allegations of anti-establishment may have been levied against KKR, in that they were disrupting the lives of C-suite professionals (and some company board members) in a publicly traded company, but they certainly were never called socialist or communist. KKR was simply working within the capitalist system and following the rules of that system in seeking to maximize return on investment.

Another example can be taken from an altogether different cultural perspective and financial product – venture capital. When Silicon Valley talks about "disrupting" an industry, the person (or firm) that disrupts that targeted industry is viewed as an entrepreneurial genius. No better example of this exists than Jeff Bezos at Amazon. How many small, medium and large-scale bookstores around the United States and the world have reduced the size of their operations or gone completely out of business because of Jeff Bezos? Have you ever heard Jeff be called a radical, a socialist or a communist? No. Why not?

Because Jeff worked within an "acceptable" legal and financial framework (venture investing) to disrupt an industry (in the beginning brick & mortar bookstores). Neither KKR nor Jeff Bezos were "outsiders."

The KKR case occurred 30 years ago. Amazon received its first seed money in 1994, raised a Series A round from Kleiner Perkins of USD 8 million in June of 1996 and had its initial public offering (IPO) in May of 1997. That is over 20 years ago.

The proposal being outlined in this book for fan empowerment and for fan and community membership/ownership of football clubs, may elicit from some very conservative elements of U.S. and Canadian society, the label of radical, socialist or communist.

Unlike in the two examples mentioned above, the proposal here is to allow people who are completely outside the top 1/10 of 1% of the wealthy, to become member/owners of football clubs.

This applies to people who have never held a membership/ownership interest in anything. We are targeting hard-core grassroots football supporters, regardless of ethnic background or income, regardless of whether you live in the city, the suburbs or the country.

As "outsiders" part of our preparation is education. Remember that education is the antidote to fake news. Education is the first step to understanding why labels like capitalist, socialist and communist are used.

Our goal is to disrupt the industry sector of football in the USA and Canada.

That football industry sector today in the USA is controlled by the top 1/10 of 1% of the wealthy. There are no "outsiders."

What we are talking about is opening up football and in particular the member-ownership of football clubs, to the entire socio-economic pyramid below the top 1/10 of 1%. Billionaires and millionaires will be welcomed with open arms, but so will factory workers, taxi and Über drivers and people who flip burgers at McDonald's or who serve expressos at Starbucks.

3.2 Juxtaposing American Football and Football

The general consensus around the country and the assumption taken often times in the press is that sports are neutral non-political activity, both for athletes and spectators/consumers, with no particular sociological or political agenda or impact.

This explains at least partially the uproar surrounding Colin Kaepernick. What few commentators talk about is the subliminal sociological and political message inherent in the very game, rules and management of American football. The NFL conveys a very powerful yet rarely discussed message to society and it has done so for decades.

American football is a violent game of territorial conquest, with a strict emphasis on following orders (each play) and a penchant for one leader (the quarterback) who sits atop the chain of command on the field. The quarterback's decision-making in turn is managed by coaches – in essence a set of generals who never enter the fray, but who control the decision-making on the field via "orders" that are strategically arrived at on the sidelines and then communicated to and applied by the quarterback. Every player on the team has a specific role to execute for each play. American football is a classic case of top-down management.

As a sport American football is as close as we have come to the consciousness and management paradigm of the military (a philosophical perspective and praxis that has been applied for several centuries in our society from education to politics to the business world). It should be no surprise then that the NFL was the focus of a dispute about the national anthem. The national anthem is after all, about war.

In this mindset of top-down control, thinking on the part of a "subordinate," much less outright protest, however measured or peaceful, is grounds for insubordination.

When discussing American football, Darwin is rarely mentioned, but he is everywhere. The NFL's supposed meritocracy, is the idea of the survival of the fittest with a gloss. Hierarchical superiority and the ability to command and give orders and have those orders obeyed without questioning is American football's mantra. Democracy is nowhere to be found. Wealthy NFL owners and wealth generally in the United States is Darwinian proof and justification for a few to sit above the masses and give orders from the commanding heights. And if necessary, democracy be damned. At least this is the self-serving interpretation of Darwin at work.

Football, on the other hand, couldn't be more different. If American football is a laboriously crafted classical music score in several movements, football is jazz, or rock n' roll, bossa nova, samba or salsa or some combination of all of these – it is a jam session of pure unadulterated improvisation. Everyone is a general.

Or everyone is a plebe. It makes no difference. The coach is more maestro than general.

The reason it is called *the beautiful game* has to do with what cannot be seen. Everyone irrespective of class, race, creed or orientation can understand football's language, but the language is not conveyed by speech. Football originates in the realm of the telepathic. The greatest teams intuitively carve, sculpt, paint, engineer and design as one mind and the absolute best of them do it as an expression of their sacred resonance with the audience, their fans. It is here that beauty is closer to the eternal than victory.

Football reminds us that there is another mind – beyond the one we possess and manage in our day-to-day affairs. It is our connection to a higher Self. The beauty created on the field is a lasting collective imprint of that Self and cannot be realized without the earth's direct participation. That is why the game for any serious artist and any serious appreciator of the art form can only be played on grass.

All football fans know that there are other laws beyond those that we experience in day-to-day concrete physical reality. The field of play is simply a stage for the metaphysical.

In actuality, Darwin's notion of evolution (a term not used in his classic work *The Origin of Species* (1859)) is an inseparable part of deeper and broader perspectives on self/Self, other and planet/cosmos, a continually penetrating ever-expanding spectrum of consciousness. You might call evolution more education. Where is American football on that spectrum? Where is football? What are we evolving away from? And as a species what are we evolving towards?

3.3 Taking Football Back From the Left and the Right

Suffice it to say that we want to challenge the thesis that sports are apolitical. And we want to do this on behalf of football fans everywhere. Fans and communities should be able to own and control or at least participate in the control of football clubs. Wealth should not be a barrier to entry. This stance by definition carries political, sociological and economic considerations.

Crowdfunding and legislation in support of it clearly indicates that the trend (and the technology) is on our side.

In this chapter we will provide some tools to position you the fan intellectually and subsequently practically to take on the responsibility of football ownership and management.

The ultimate goal of this book and movement is to create a one-stop shop for all fan's and/or communities' needs regarding how to create, sustain and grow a football club.

One of those tools is how to defend yourself from political criticism from both the left and the right. Football offers a third way.

The criticism from the left is that all sports and entertainment is part of a larger scheme of the capitalist agenda, to maintain you (the fan and citizen) as a largely unconscious spoke in the larger wheel of mass consumerism. Marketing's specific and only purpose is to keep you buying product with the fewest possible questions other than the questions as to product style, color and pricing.

With the advance of the Internet, smart phones, social media and peer-to-peer (P2P), along with global movements like climate change (which regardless of your beliefs forces at least the beginning of critical thinking) not only are products being questioned as to their quality and efficacy, but they are also being questioned in terms of whether that product is even needed and more seriously what is that product's impact on society and the planet?

That is why placing football clubs at the epicenter of community organizing, community building and community revitalization is so important. As a result, football becomes by definition more than a sport – it becomes a cultural phenomenon and a catalyst for change.

So when someone challenges you by saying that, by participating in the building of a football club you are simply contributing to the further alienation of the masses, the response is that we are building community and in the process waking people up as to their role in not just their neighborhood as citizens, but as to their vested interest in the revitalization of democracy in our society.

The critique from the right will be along the lines of challenging football as a legitimate sport – that it is not "manly" because women play it as much as men do. Or that football is boring because it is "low scoring" and true Americans like scoring and measuring achievement, particularly to prove that someone is better than someone else. Or they may even say that football is anti-American because it requires that everyone work together to score. In that sense it is either socialist or worse communist. Football they will argue degrades and puts a damper on individual achievement and debases the notion of individual stars so common in the other team sports in the United States.

Of course the idea of star power in football is easily refuted. The other ideas of football being less than masculine because women play it or that it is boring because it is low scoring are worth a response.

Football is popular globally for a simple reason – you do not have to be a great athlete to play it and play it decently. Its popularity, therefore, is due in part to the fact that the tens of millions of people who have played it or witnessed it up close, realize the tremendous beauty of the sport when a genius applies their craft. And that genius can be a man or a woman. That is why Marta or Messi or Cristiano Ronaldo or Neymar are so idolized, because they have taken what is arguably the most difficult ball skills sport and made it look effortless and elegant. The low scoring for those who have played and/or know the game is not an issue – it is the mental, physical and even spiritual interaction of two clubs and the culture that surrounds the challenge of confronting an adversary on the field that carries the drama. The more delicate issue is the accusation that football is somehow socialist or even communist.

The first rebuttal is that American football, namely the NFL, is the most socialist sport in the United States, because the NFL teams literally split the revenues evenly irrespective of performance, franchise value or market size.

An average NFL game lasts 3 hours and 12 minutes, but if you tally up the time when the ball is actually in play, the action amounts to a mere 11 minutes. There are more than 100 commercials per game. The entire game is commanded hierarchically by one man, a quarterback (who in turns takes his orders from the coaches on the sidelines) with each player in a given role for a given play. The cognitive, that is thinking on an individual level, has been fully substituted for following orders and regimentation.

In addition, American football's values reinforce sexist stereotypes, is quintessentially male chauvinist and clearly maintains violence as its core operating principal.

Your response must include as well that society is evolving to less hierarchical schemes of working together and that technology is flattening the prior corporate and militaristic reporting lines allowing for more peer-to-peer value creation. This trend is global and irreversible.

Lastly, is it a coincidence that football is the world's sport and that American football is limited to the USA?

Tell them that if they want to buck global trends they are free to do so, but rest assured in supporting American football, they are choosing a train that is at the end of the line (baseball, hockey and basketball interesting enough support the cooperative position more than the hierarchical one).

We are in difficult times. Our country is divided and appears to be adrift without a compass.

Football is not a complete solution, but it can be structured to be a partial solution to make our lives better and more meaningful, particularly in our rural, suburban and inner-city communities.

In order to prepare ourselves to deal not only with the opportunity that football presents, but also with the criticism we will inevitably receive, I want to recommend that you review the following readings and videos.

My suggestion with the books, videos/movies and other information cited here is that you ideally read and see the content in the company of friends or other interested parties. And please, after you read and see the content pass it along to others.

Crowdocracy

Crowdocracy: The End of Politics, by Alan Watkins and Iman Stratenus.

Crowdocracy (a play on the words crowdfunding and democracy) is a clarion call for people everywhere to take control of their lives, their communities and their governments. Watkins and Stratenus argue that the Internet and technology generally, have brought us to the point of being able to "take back" our democracy via technology. That means self-empowerment at the local, regional and national level. It is a rekindling of grassroots democratic impulses.

Crowdocracy embraces key components of personal and neighborhood revitalization and makes a strong case that diverse large groups are more insightful than individual genius or small groups of so-called experts.

This renewed and technologically empowered vision of democracy is at the heart and soul of the football club concept being employed in this book.

Saving Capitalism

Robert Reich's film *Saving Capitalism* (available on Netflix).

This documentary provides a close-up look at how democracy and capitalism have been undermined by vested interests. The same phenomenon is occurring with football in the USA and Canada.

The Vietnam War

The Vietnam War: A Film by Ken Burns and Lynn Novick (available on PBS).

This is one of the most powerful documentaries that you will see regarding war, government deception and the role of the United States in global affairs. It juxtaposes the challenges and the conflicts that come with questioning authority, with the connection between government and the truth, and the proper role of citizenship in a functioning democracy.

Understanding that war, understanding those who supported it and those who opposed it, is essential homework to grasp the hurdles that will be presented to football and to those who support football becoming a or the dominant sport in the USA.

League of Denial

League of Denial: The NFL's Concussion Crisis (available from PBS).

This is a powerful documentary about the NFL's concussion crisis, how the neurogenerative disease chronic traumatic encephalopathy (CTE) was discovered, how it evolved and how the NFL and NFL players reacted to the devastation involved with the crisis.

As will be discussed at length below, the role of the NFL and its influence on football (as distinguished from the NFL's own American football) carries serious implications for the future of football, not only in the USA but in the Americas.

Concussion

Concussion is Will Smith's adaptation based on the incredible true David vs. Goliath story of American immigrant Dr. Bennet Omalu, the brilliant forensic neuropathologist who made the first discovery of CTE, an American football-related brain trauma in a professional American football player and fought for the truth to be known. Omalu's emotional quest puts him at dangerous odds with one of the most powerful – and beloved – institutions in the United States, the NFL (available on Netflix).

Out of Their League

Out of Their League, by Dave Meggyesy.

This personal testimony to life in the NFL is timeless. Written by Dave Meggyesy about his experiences as an outside linebacker for the then St. Louis Cardinals (now the Arizona Cardinals), he chronicles the racism, the drug use, the exploitation by owners, coaches and even players and the violence. Disturbingly, the book is as relevant today as it was nearly 50 years ago (it was published in 1970 and reissued in 2005). It confirms how little the NFL and its owners have changed.

The Reactionary Mind

The Reactionary Mind: From Edmund Burke to Donald Trump (2nd Edition), by Corey Robin.

Corey Robin, a professor at Brooklyn College, has updated his prior exploration of the history and evolution of conservative thought. This is a must read for anyone interested in understanding today's Trumpian world and the likely responses to the proposals here, in what will inevitably be called by some, the socialization of sports.

The Road to Serfdom

The Road to Serfdom, by F.A. Hayek.

The Road to Serfdom is a classic conservative text that concludes that central economic planning (a hallmark of socialist ideology, think the old Soviet Union) not only does not work but it also sets the stage for eventual totalitarian and fascist rule.

Would Hayek support Major League Soccer's position regarding central planning and in particular its stance against promotion and relegation?

Interestingly, some of the basic tenets of The Road to Serfdom, if they were applied today to the political and economic situation in the United States, would lead to a conservative (Hayekian) deconstruction of conservative economic policy. Would Hayek support the tyranny of the top 1/10 of 1% of the wealthy, their lobbyists, and the undermining of democratic processes by deep-pocketed conservative contributors and lobbyists?

A fascinating book and one worth reading given the current political climate and the challenges football is facing.

Milton Friedman on Monopoly Power: https://www.youtube.com/watch?v=tdLBzfFGFQU

Friedman's basic thesis is that not only are monopolies not a good thing but when we look behind the scenes there is often a governmental rule or agency supporting the very monopoly in question. In the case of the MLS monopoly, Friedman is right on. The quasi-governmental role that FIFA and U.S. Soccer play assures MLS's monopoly, and the U.S. government's Internal Revenue Service (IRS) is the reason that MLS has survived for over two decades with a chronic set of losses every year for more than two decades.

Up From Eden

Up From Eden: A Transpersonal View of Human Evolution, by Ken Wilber and especially Chapter 19: Republicans, Democrats, and Mystics.

Ken Wilber is an American philosopher. He is often called the father of Integral Theory. Integral Theory is the attempt to provide the first truly comprehensive global framework for all aspects of knowledge, particularly the Western and Eastern philosophical traditions.

Integral theory ultimately places conservatism, liberalism and all political, social and economic theory on a spectrum of consciousness. This in turn led

Wilber to develop the 4 Quadrant analysis of the human evolutionary predicament.

Analyzing sports through an Integral Theory lens begins the process of linking sports and the aspects and intricacies of each sport along the lines of individual and collective consciousness and their evolution. There are significant implications for football in the United States and where football fits on the spectrum of consciousness.

For more, Google Integral Theory.

Homo Ludens

Homo Ludens: A Study of the Play Element in Culture, by Johan Huizinga.

Homo Ludens is a classic historical appraisal of the role of play in society from the Greeks up to the 20th Century. "Homo ludens" or "Man Who Plays" provides historical, social and political lens to chronicle the importance of play in civilization.

This book will help shed light on the evolutionary importance of football in the USA in the 21st Century.

The Culture Industry

The Culture Industry: Selected Essays on Mass Culture, by Theodore Adorno.

Adorno, a leading member of the Frankfurt School, was an ardent critic of the use of culture (as an industry) to reproduce the status quo of a society controlled by industrial capitalism.

This Frankfurt School thesis carries serious implications for football (or any sport) and its relation to the entrenched business interests who control the means of production, as well as the imposed and often unquestioned vision and values of a given society.

The Culture Industry and Participatory Audiences

The Culture Industry and Participatory Audiences, by Emma Keltie.

Digital technology and the Internet in particular are changing the prior one-way relationship that 20th Century media (particularly radio and TV) imposed on consumers. Initially, all consumers did simply that – consume whatever was presented to them. This passive receipt of the message (whatever the message) reinforced not only the status quo of capitalist society, but also reinforced the claim to power than investors and interested stakeholders had in the means of production.

In the late 20th Century and the early 21st Century technology has evolved communications from a one-way consumption model, to a two-way interactive model. The content received is now being placed in the hands of consumers who in turn can and do become producers. How much of the original status quo message remains?

In truth the two-way interactive model is a precursor to an already existing and evolving omni-channel real-time peer-to-peer (P2P) model that lends itself to more sophisticated forms of group-driven cross-pollinated mass consumption.

The question is what can individual and group consciousness contribute collaboratively to off-set, counter-balance and even overthrow the old traditional consumptive message which maintains the status quo?

This contextualizes the challenge before football in the USA and Canada. Can football raise consciousness and sustainably restructure itself to overthrow the yoke that has been placed upon it? Can fans and communities not only build and maintain football clubs, but can they rebuild and revitalize via those clubs, the very neighborhoods in which they live in a non-exploitative way?

Oprah Winfrey's Speech at the Golden Globe Awards:

http://variety.com/2018/film/news/oprahs-entire-golden-globes-speech-1202656450/amp/

Oprah's message could not be more timely. The equal role of women is absolutely crucial to the healthy functional future of our society and for both men's and women's football.

Football is on its way to becoming the #1 sport in the United States in terms of the number of participants.

The ultimate goal of becoming #1 in the world of football has already been attained by the USWNT. The fact that no one wants to face, much less admit, is that women from the grassroots to the top of the football pyramid hold the future of the game in their hands for the men as well.

The dysfunctionality and chaos of the USA's football pyramid was not created by women. Without women being totally involved in the revamping of this sport in our rural communities, in our suburbs and in our urban centers and inner-city neighborhoods, the proposals contained in The Football Manifesto will not come to pass. Women represent the mechanism to bring order out of the chaos.

For those of you who would like to begin immediately and directly with statistically-driven football themes, Deloitte provides ample coverage of European football clubs with their annual Football Money League (FML) reports.

These reports are available on the Deloitte website for downloading. Also available for download are Deloitte's Annual Review of Football Finance reports, which take a broader perspective on the performance of the Big 5 football leagues and other European leagues.

UEFA and the Bundesliga also produce annual reports about their overall financial performance that are available for download.

PART II: CURRENT STATE OF FOOTBALL IN THE USA AND GLOBALLY

"But now MLS starts to sound like a pyramid scheme. You can fund a loss-making enterprise from the entrance fees of new buyers for a while, but without making money, the only reason for doing this would be glory, not profits. Americans constantly tell me that owners of sport franchises in the US will insist on making money. If that really is the case, then I predict that MLS will collapse, and probably sooner rather than later."

--- Professor Stefan Szymanski

Understanding the current state of football requires an exploration of attitudes, policy stances and concrete steps that have been taken in the past. How we got here and why, is just as important as planning to create a new dynamic future.

The purpose of this section of the book is to dimension the challenge before us.

Being Amongst the Best in the World v. Being #1 in the World

The 2006 men's World Cup, which held in Germany, was viewed by German football authorities as a harsh lesson and stark expression of Germany's fall from global greatness. Germany took third place by defeating Portugal 3-1.

After winning the World Cup in 1990, Germany made only one more WC final in 2002 where it lost to Brazil 2-0 (the first time in the entire history of the World Cup that Brazil and Germany had faced off).

Germany's European championships also told the story of the country's decline. After winning the 1996 European championship, the closest Germany came again was runner-up to Spain's great side in 2008. But by 2008, the restructuring of German football was already in full swing.

After 2006, German football authorities convened and put together a new plan of action to restore Germany to its rightful place amongst the world's great football powers. The goal was to become #1 in the world. As we all know, that goal was realized in 2014, when Germany won the World Cup in Brazil.

In the United States by contrast, being #1 in the world of football is never discussed.

The discussion is always couched around the idea that at some point in the future the USA will be "amongst the best in the world."

That kind of a goal is no goal at all. It is simply a distraction.

It is the kind of statement that is made by someone who at bottom either does not want you to succeed or does not believe that you can succeed. It is the statement of someone who does not have your best interests at heart. Don't trust them.

The only worthy goal of the USA is to be #1 in the world.

To do that the USA must meet and then exceed the global standard of excellence for football national teams, leagues and clubs.

At the national team level, the United States Women's National Team (USWNT) has met that standard and exceeded it. The men have not. We will discuss the reasons for why this is the case at some length below.

At the level of leagues and clubs, however, neither the men nor the women in the USA meet the global standard of excellence.

Some may say that the USA needs to do what Germany did after 2006. In short, get its house in order. But by 2006 Germany had already won three World Cups and been World Cup runners-up 4 times. What the USA needs to do first is build the house.

Rumors began circulating after the USA's failure to qualify for the 2018 World Cup in Russia, that some entrepreneurs were considering a "losers World Cup," to be staged in the USA during 2018, given that Chile, Holland, Italy and the USA had all failed to qualify.

Having accomplished nothing in men's football on the global stage in modern times and having no football culture in the USA to fall back on (a culture that would have brought with it a passionate embarrassment at the current state of affairs), the only response that some in the USA can muster is "well let's make some money off of our dire predicament!"

If there is one lesson to be learned about not qualifying for World Cup 2018, it is that arrogance will get you nowhere. The USA needs to be humble. That is the only solid foundation worthy of the task in front of us.

Until you get to be #1 keep your head down and respect your elders (and after you get to be #1 you keep your head down and respect your elders).

At this point, the USA isn't worthy enough to stage a loser's World Cup (we have accomplished nothing globally that puts us even close to the company of Italy, the Netherlands or Chile). Only someone who has no clue about football culture and no respect for or interest in building it, would contemplate such an idea.

What FIFA's Monopoly Means

Despite the controversy surrounding them, former FIFA Presidents João Havelange (1974 – 1998 as FIFA President) and Sepp Blatter (1998 – 2015 as FIFA President), both represented a strong counter-balance to European hegemony in the football world. Together they were in power for 41 consecutive years (despite their strong support of Africa, Asia and Latin America, they also witnessed the rise of UEFA and European football and the migration of the world's best footballers to European leagues and clubs).

In 2015, that balance of power changed with the election of Gianni Infantino. Infantino is a former senior official at the Union of European Football Associations (UEFA), the dominant football governing body for Europe, and a FIFA sanctioned monopoly.

Today, Europe is the epicenter of the football world. The world's richest clubs, the world's richest tournaments, the highest player salaries, the largest media rights, commercial and stadia-related revenue generation all happen in Europe. UEFA is at the core of this – it is the foundation of an annual multi-billion dollar industry based in Europe.

Which brings us to the Big 5: England, Germany, Spain, Italy and France are the leading football nations of Europe. According to Deloitte, these countries collectively generate the equivalent of USD 13-14 billion annually in football revenues.

For one month every four years, with the FIFA Men's World Cup, other non-European football powers like Brazil and Argentina appear on the global radar screens of football fans worldwide, but for the other three years and eleven months, Europe is the center of the world. This unipolar concentration of football power carries serious implications for the future of football in the USA.

The fact that Mr. Infantino, a former UEFA senior official now runs FIFA, complicates as we shall see, the current crisis and malaise in football in the USA, which is best exemplified by the recent failure of the USMNT to qualify for the 2018 World Cup.

If you are a football fan in the USA, you must be concerned not only with the World Cup (for two months every four years), but with the state and quality of the professional leagues and clubs in the USA (for the other three years and ten months).

Obviously, an analysis of FIFA can ill-afford to ignore the role of the United States Department of Justice (DOJ), in the FIFA corruption scandal. But for the DOJ, it is safe to say that Mr. Infantino would not be where he is today.

We can also say, that but for the support of U.S. Soccer, and in particular Sunil Gulati (a member of the FIFA Executive Committee) in the 2015 vote for the new FIFA President, Gianni Infantino might not be President.

What is completely off the radar screen of bloggers, the mainstream press and fans in the USA, is the key role that MLS Commissioner Don Garber played in that same FIFA election.

What does it say about the current state of football, when the USA has positioned itself to play a key role in the election of FIFA's President?

How and why did this occur in a country that is supposedly so unimpressed with the beautiful game and so unaccomplished on the field?

Monopolies are the same everywhere. They are resistant to change. They abhor competition. And they will do everything in their power to maintain the status quo.

So far, we have briefly addressed in general terms two monopolies.

The first was the monopoly of the Big 4 in the USA and Canada.

The second was the monopoly of FIFA and UEFA in Europe.

There is a third monopoly power to be addressed. The third monopoly power is Major League Soccer (MLS), a monopoly conferred by U.S. Soccer, which is itself a monopoly, as FIFA's representative in the USA.

For organizations that supposedly have only the best interests of footballers in the USA as their mandate, U.S. Soccer and MLS have adopted certain policy positions and taken certain actions, which run counter to the best interests of the sport from any objective standpoint (this will be explored below).

Certain U.S. Soccer officials may dispute the claims made here. They may respond that what is "in the best interest of the sport," is entirely subjective or even more forcefully, they may say that as the FIFA representative for the USA, it is their call and their call alone as to what qualifies as "in the best interest."

Here is the bottom line: given their overlapping policies and actions there is ample room to question U.S. Soccer's and MLS's motivations.

We cannot read former U.S. Soccer President Sunil Gulati's mind. Nor can we read the mind of MLS Commissioner Don Garber. New U.S. Soccer President Carlos Cordeiro (as of February 2018) was considered an establishment candidate – there to reinforce the existing policy regime of his predecessors. We also cannot read the minds of U.S. Soccer-MLS/SUM supporters inside and outside of their respective organizations.

Nevertheless, their public positions and their actions beg the question – who do they really work for?

And just as importantly, we must recognize, that U.S. Soccer and MLS are structurally a part of the problem.

It is structure, meaning the current institutional framework of football in the USA (i.e., the pyramid) and not simply and only personalities, that is the problem.

To be crystal clear, the organizational structure in question cannot be separated from the policy stances at issue.

Practically, this means that running for the position of President of U.S. Soccer and winning, may be an illusion. The problem we face has been structured into the very institutional fabric and mentality of U.S. Soccer and its supporters.

The same thing holds true for Don Garber and MLS. The obvious difference being that there is no obvious entry point into changing MLS, unless you buy yourself in as an investor-owner of a team – a move that is self-defeating from the standpoint of true change.

One of the assumptions about the position of President of U.S. Soccer, is that a new President would be positioned to impose promotion and relegation on the entire football pyramid, including MLS.

Promotion and relegation (a topic to be discussed below) is an interesting idea. However, it is not the panacea many assume, much less a complete solution.

In addition, there is no guarantee that U.S. Soccer as a deliberative body would agree to promotion and relegation simply because U.S. Soccer has a new President in Carlos Cordeiro. Nor is there any reason to believe MLS would support such a change – not to mention supporting a candidate for President of U.S. Soccer with such views (it is common knowledge that both Don Garber and Sunil Gulati, while he was President of U.S. Soccer, came out publicly against promotion and relegation). At this point, we have to assume that Carlos Cordeiro, who was clearly supported by MLS in the election, is against promotion and relegation.

Anyone in the world of institutional and organizational change knows that resistance to change and managing that resistance to change is the structural, cognitive and emotional challenge of any and all change agents (either internal or external change agents).

There are well-established vested interests both inside U.S. Soccer-MLS/SUM and outside that do not want to see change occur.

The painful truth is that there are many people currently involved with football as administrators and as owners both domestically and internationally, who do not want to see the USA reach its full potential and become a dominant global power.

Chapter 4 will drill down into three key monopolies that impact football in the United States and will explore in more depth one of those monopolies, the NFL (American football) and its relationship to football.

Chapter 5 will dive deep into MLS.

Chapter 6 will evaluate what is being called U.S. Soccer's War, and its role in having created (along with MLS) the current state of football in the USA.

Chapter 7 will provide a picture of the current state of football in the rest of the world.

FIFA, UEFA, U.S. Soccer-MLS/SUM, the NFL and the Big 5 can individually and collectively be considered (or not) the "football powers that be," including the relationships that each body has developed with the global media industry, construction, apparel suppliers, Wall Street, government, etc.

FIFA's award of the 1994 World Cup to the United States came with a condition subsequent. Namely, that the USA would found and grow a professional football league. This commitment was agreed to well before 1994 and those who involved themselves in the formation of MLS took full advantage of the opportunity.

No one can fault them for structuring football the best way they saw fit. No one can fault them for the current state of football in the USA. And no one can fault them for not wanting to change. Nor can we fault them for being self-interested. U.S. Soccer-MLS/SUM after all is their baby.

What is not their baby and what they have no right to claim dominion over – is football itself.

CHAPTER 4: THE ROLE OF THREE (3) OVERLAPPING AND INTERLOCKING MONOPOLIES AND HOW THEY WORK IN CONJUNCTION TO GUARANTEE THAT THE USA MAINTAINS ITS GLOBALLY INFERIOR STATUS IN MEN'S FOOTBALL

"The NFL is a natural cartel that exerts major monopoly power over its die-hard fans, media outlets and general taxpayers. By artificially limiting the number of franchises, the league is able to maximize revenues, profits, franchise value and expansion and relocation fees while playing thinly veiled extortion games for public stadium subsidies."
--- Professor John Vrooman
"How do you make the game safer? You don't play."
---Brett Favre, NFL Hall of Famer
"As FIFA President, I have to care . . . about having also challengers to the European associations and leagues."
--- Gianni Infantino, FIFA President, in an ESPN interview shortly after the U.S. Soccer Presidential elections in February 2018

4.1 Three (3) Monopolies Impacting Football in the USA Today

In the global scheme of men's football the United States of America is a developing world nation.

How did this happen in the richest country in the world – a country that has four major leagues (the Big 4) where each league sets the global standard of excellence in their respective sport?

Why and how has the USA been unable to develop the global standard of excellence in football?

The answer to these questions can be found deeply embedded in the relationship between three monopoly powers:

(1) UEFA-FIFA,

(2) U.S. Soccer-MLS/SUM, and

(3) The National Football League (NFL).

Think of each of these monopolies as a separate leg in an equilateral triangle.

Leg (1) representing the Big 5 football nations of Europe generates roughly USD 13-14 billion in revenue annually and is the center of the football world. The engine and glue that holds these nations together is the UEFA-FIFA monopoly.

Leg (2) representing the U.S. Soccer-MLS/SUM monopoly (conferred by FIFA) represents annual revenue of approximately USD 500 million, with MLS/SUM publicly acknowledging that it is generating annual losses of USD 100-150 million.

Leg (3) representing the NFL monopoly generates approximately USD 14 billion in annual revenue.

Leg (2), the weaker leg of the triangle, U.S. Soccer-MLS/SUM, is not acting independently. It is being squeezed by Leg (1) and Leg (3). In fact, the triangle is not balanced and equilateral, it is an isosceles triangle with Leg (2)'s growth and extension severely limited and we will argue purposefully so.

Leg (2) is exercising it monopoly status at the behest of and for the benefit of Leg (1) and Leg (3).

The assumption is that Leg (2), U.S. Soccer-MLS/SUM, aside from the conferral of monopoly status by FIFA, operates as its own monopoly without much guidance or influence by FIFA (and supposedly no influence from UEFA) or the NFL. That assumption is erroneous.

The U.S. Soccer-MLS/SUM monopoly is a potent force *against* the rise of the USA to global football prominence. There is ample evidence to support that conclusion.

The evidence manifests itself across the entire football pyramid in the USA:

- A weighted voting system inside U.S. Soccer which has disenfranchised youth football and disproportionately empowered MLS/SUM
- The Yedlin litigation and the issue of Solidarity Payments now before FIFA's Dispute Resolution Chamber (DRC)
- Pay-to-Play which excludes tens if not hundreds of thousands of potentially talented youth in our rural areas and in our inner-cities, ultimately keeping the game elitist and suburban
- Three independent nationwide youth organizations that compete against one another
- Coaching too much and too early and then not enough plus sub-par scouting
- The total undermining of the notion of a football meritocracy by not providing equal pay for women (when in fact based on performance and merit the women deserve at least what the men get if not more)
- The farce of the divisional system in the professional ranks, which masks the real intent of the U.S. Soccer-MLS/SUM monopoly to preserve the status quo of one and only one top-tier major professional league complemented by one or several minor leagues (the flip side of the promotion-relegation debate)
- A professional league in MLS that for 20+ years has prized mediocrity over the global standard of league and club excellence

- A league in MLS that prides itself on Division I status, when in truth it is at best a second division or third division league by global standards
- Average MLS stadium size of roughly 22-23,000 after the full build-out of MLS's proposed 28 team expansion – virtually locks-in MLS' long-term mediocrity, given the fact that 22-23,000 is considerably below the average stadium size of the U.K. and German second divisions
- An MLS salary cap *per team* that is the equivalent of the average salary *per player* amongst the best clubs in the EPL and Bundesliga
- Annual combined revenue at MLS (including all MLS teams and SUM) that is less than the annual revenue of Real Madrid
- A TV contract for MLS that is 1/26 of the EPL's TV contract
- A uniform branding strategy for the entire league that classically commodifies the sport
- A single entity business model of centralized management which works well to control expenses but which has failed miserably on the revenue side of the equation when compared to our global benchmarks
- After over two decades of consecutive annual losses (now publicly admitted to be USD 100-

150MM/year) a commitment to the status quo for the foreseeable future

These are facts.

Despite the troubling current state of football in the USA, we are faced with another fact: the USA is the only country in the world that in the short-term is fully capable of threatening Europe's global football hegemony.

By short-term, I mean that within a 5 to 10-year timeframe (or less), with a radically different well-structured approach, the USA could rival the strongest nations in football, both in Europe and in Latin America.

Remember, Europe is the absolute center of the football world. With the USA as a legitimate football power, the balance of power would shift.

U.S. Soccer-MLS/SUM is structured to make sure that that shift in the balance of power does not happen.

4.2 USA Football as a Threat to European Football Hegemony

The USA as a global football power would have consequences. The first impact on Europe would be in the revenue category of talent management.

Ask yourself a question: what would Europe be today in global football without talent from Latin America and Africa?

Without that imported talent, would you be waking up at 6am on Saturday morning?

If the USA became a world-class football power, a global shift in Europe's centrifugal force, the sucking power of talent from the rest of the world, particularly from Latin America and Africa, would be disrupted.

International talent (or at least a portion of it) would begin to flow to the USA.

This is the reason and justification for UEFA-FIFA wanting to maintain the status quo in the USA.

4.3 USA Football as a Threat to the NFL

In relevant juxtaposition, if the USA became a world-class football power, the same issue of a potential talent drain would apply inside the USA as well, however, in a very different way.

The relationship between Leg (2) and Leg (3) of our triangle, namely the relationship between U.S. Soccer-MLS/SUM and the NFL is hardly, if ever spoken of.

Our argument here is that with the transformation of the USA into a legitimate top-tier football power on the global stage, there would be short, medium and long-term talent drain. Youth now in the American football pipeline would migrate to the football pipeline.

Given the NFL's penchant for long-term planning, we must assume that the NFL has reached the same conclusion with respect to football's threat to American football.

Not only that, upon reaching that conclusion no doubt years ago, the evidence indicates that the NFL acted to protect its interests.

What better way to do that than to invest in and control the growth and evolution of football from its inception. MLS's single-entity format does exactly that.

Nevertheless, and wholly apart from the question of football's threat to American football, the NFL has created its own set of challenges that amount to a self-generated undermining of its own cash cow.

The bottom line is that American football is violent, and the NFL is destroying itself alone and from within.

The concussion issue will not go away. Other issues like serious injuries in practice as well as games (increasingly to the league's stars) drug use/abuse, domestic violence, crime, the national anthem, etc. have worked together to undermine the NFL and the feeder system underneath it. The impact of concussions on youth, high school and even NCAA American football has been dramatic.

Pop Warner attendance has entered a steady and likely unstoppable decline. High school numbers are down as well. The Ivy League's entire NCAA Division I American football program now bans hitting and tackling in practice, saving the potential damage for game day only.

4.4 The NFL's Motivation for Wanting to Maintain the USA's Football Status Quo

70% of the NFL's players are African-American, while African-Americans represent 13-14% of the overall population. American football has long been a ticket out of the ghetto.

Sports generally have been a principal climbing mechanism (along with education) on the USA's socio-economic ladder of success.

Money, long-term financial security and fame have been at the heart and soul of professional team sports in the USA (and Canada) for decades.

These are the principle motivating factors for the "great athlete," and this explains why athletes concentrate and migrate their skill sets to a given sport or sports while they are young.

At some point, usually in their early to mid-teens, the best athletes choose to focus their attention on one sport in the hope of securing a college scholarship or a professional contract.

The NBA (75% of the players are African-American), Major League Baseball and the National Hockey League, along with the NFL all operate and benefit from the elaborate feeder system below the professional level.

Amongst the Big 4, however, the NFL stands to be the league that will be impacted the most by football's evolution toward world-class status.

The best athletes will still choose basketball as their #1 sport. The NBA will continue to be the highest paid sport per player in the world.

The impact that football has on basketball therefore will be negligible at best. The same is true for hockey, in that the NHL's current feeder system will only be marginally impacted by football's evolution. Baseball is harder to judge, but as time goes by and the NFL paradigm of concussions worsens, there will be added pressure on young athletes to reconsider baseball as an option.

It is, however, American football and its feeder system that will be impacted the greatest by football's evolution in the USA toward the global standard of excellence.

In 2017, the average NFL annual salary ranged from USD 2.07MM (SF 49ers) to USD 2.99 (Oakland Raiders). This is the lowest average amongst the Big 4.

The average career of an NFL player is best understood by position: quarterbacks: 4.4 years; cornerbacks: 2.94 years; wide receivers: 2.81 years and running backs: 2.57 years. The overall league average for an NFL career is 3.3 years. [1]

In a high school athlete's mind and in the mind of his parents, the anticipated multi-million dollar a year contracts that the NFL stands for, are increasingly being viewed as potentially not worth it, particularly if there are other sporting options.

Skilled positions were chosen here as the most likely option for athlete migration from American football to football.

Football, like basketball, is a ball skills sport. Therefore, the better athletes will naturally migrate to football and away from American football as the crisis engulfing the NFL (a crisis entirely of its own making) worsens.

Of the Big 4 sports, the NFL already pays the worst and it also carries the highest risk of a career ending injury.

When football becomes a legitimate global force in the USA, you can expect a migration of untapped athletic talent to football that was heretofore focused on American football and the other Big 4 sports.

African-Americans in particular as well as Hispanics, Asians and urban ethnic groups (particularly those immigrants from Europe with strong football traditions) will gravitate toward football in large numbers when football becomes world-class and begins reaching world-class salary levels.

The allure of playing against the best talent in the world and having global exposure and all that that brings financially and otherwise (which is something that American football cannot offer) allows us to understand why the NFL is very concerned and very involved in controlling U.S. Soccer-MLS/SUM.

This puts Solidarity Payments and Pay-to-Play in a new light.

Both the Yedlin case and Solidarity Payments (or the lack thereof) and Pay-to-Play, which is the principal mechanism for keeping the game of football out of the inner-city (i.e., ghettos and barrios) both play right into the status quo that the NFL wants to maintain.

The policy decisions of U.S. Soccer-MLS/SUM benefit either the UEFA-FIFA monopoly or the NFL monopoly, directly or indirectly, 100% of the time.

It should come as no surprise then that MLS's salary cap *per team* began in 1996 at USD 1.6 million and for the 2018 season is USD 4.035 million per team.

If you Google the current MLS salary situation, articles will appear about Targeted Allocation Money (TAM), that is over and above the salary cap. Even with TAM, MLS is keeping salaries so low that there is absolutely no threat to the NFL's talent pipeline (or any other sport's talent pipeline).

These decisions are being made by former NFL employees who have worked for years for MLS.

Under this purposefully low payment scheme the pipeline of inner-city and low-income black high school American football talent, has absolutely no incentive to take up football at any age.

We would be remiss if we did not mention the role of the NCAA as a feeder mechanism to the NFL. Although scholarship athletes who play American football are aggressively recruited out of high school (and in some cases even before) they still do not "officially" receive money for playing American football in college.

Nevertheless, the perks available to American football players in the NCAA is substantial and often "under the table." Whether payments are funneled to their parents surreptitiously (via alums), or "in kind" payments to athletes are received (again from fanatic alumni), junior high and high school players know that they and their families will be taken care of if they play NCAA American football.

The NFL is interested in preserving that pipeline, and it has no intention of letting football interfere with it.

Here is something to think about. Estimates are that despite the counter-productive structure in the nationwide ranks of youth football in the United States, the collective annual spend is USD 5 billion. Think about what could be done if youth football in the USA were well-organized and inclusive of all sectors of society and then fully integrated with the professional level a lá Germany.

The Football Manifesto is about making that happen.

4.5 Football in the Americas as a Threat to Europe

A second and no less important consideration, is that with the USA as a legitimate global football power, it could then work in conjunction with the existing football powers in the Americas – from Mexico down to Colombia, Chile, Argentina and Brazil, to create an UEFA-like organization for the Americas, that would substitute CONCACAF and CONMEBOL, directly threatening UEFA's European hegemony.

UEFA, FIFA and the NFL all know this. Anyone can see the handwriting on the wall.

These are the motivating reasons for U.S. Soccer-MLS/SUM to avoid at all costs, the emergence of the USA as a global football power.

The football pyramid in the USA is dysfunctional from top to bottom. That dysfunction serves this larger purpose.

The fact that the U.S. Soccer-MLS/SUM monopoly has tolerated this situation for more than two decades, and managed it via policies that undermine the game, speaks volumes about their ultimate intentions.

The tendency is to simply chalk up the actions and performance of U.S. Soccer-MLS/SUM over the past 20+ years to bad business judgment.

Another analysis says that the vested interests of the MLS investor-owners are the actual cause of the problems.

Both of these conclusions are considerably wide of the mark.

The real question, the part of the equation that is the most confusing from the outside looking in, has to do with what is motivating the leadership of U.S. Soccer and MLS/SUM to work against the best interests of the sport of football in the USA?

The answer to what is motivating the leadership of U.S. Soccer and MLS/SUM is another monopoly, the National Football League.

Regardless of their claimed intentions, regardless of what may be plausibly denied, *in practice* U.S. Soccer-

MLS/SUM is operating (and has been for some time) as an NFL front.

Over the years and particularly given the weighted voting scheme at U.S. Soccer and the rigors of the single-entity requirements at MLS on investor-owners, the respective institutional frameworks and their policies have been structured in favor of the NFL. Obviously, having former NFL employees at the highest possible level in both institutions for years has been quite helpful, but as it stands both organizations are now entrenched, to such an extent, that largely independent of who leads these organizations their respective governance structures and legacy hires assure a high degree of favoritism for policy stances that benefit the interests of the NFL. This is in spite of the fact that MLS now has a majority of non-NFL owners in its ranks.

4.6 The NFL Connection

Again, the facts:

- NFL owners Robert Kraft and Lamar Hunt were amongst the original founders of MLS
- NFL owners have always held a disproportionate impact on MLS's day-to-day operations via their membership on the MLS Board of Governors

- Robert Kraft is currently the honorary chair of the 2026 World Cup Organizing Committee
- The majority of the stadia used for the 1994 World Cup were NFL stadia
- The majority of the stadia preliminarily identified for the 2026 World Cup are NFL stadia (for the games to be held in the USA in the three-country bid)
- In the early history of MLS the then ten teams were all owned by NFL owners or prospective NFL owners (Phil Anschutz who was then the leading candidate for an NFL franchise in Los Angeles owned 6 of the 10 franchises, while Hunt owned three and Kraft owned one)
- The anti-trust lawsuit known as the *Fraser* case which was filed by the MLS players against MLS, was joined in an *amicus curiae* brief by the NFL Players Association
- Sunil Gulati was formerly Deputy Commissioner at MLS, and was also employed by Robert Kraft as head of Kraft Sports Group (responsible *inter alia* for Kraft's New England Revolution franchise in MLS)
- Don Garber's entire career prior to his appointment as MLS Commissioner was with the NFL (for 16 years), in his last position he was SVP/MD for NFL International where he had responsibility for all of the NFL's business operations overseas

- Bill Peterson, former NASL Commissioner, also worked for Phil Anschutz in the management of his then multiple MLS franchises, and was also a former senior official at NFL Europe
- Steve Ross, owner of the NFL Miami Dolphins is also the owner of Relevant Sports, which working in conjunction with MLS/SUM organizes all the "friendlies" and the International Champions Cup, which brings the great European football clubs to the USA every summer
- Providence Equity, which until recently held a 20% stake in SUM (2012-2017) and has now exited, has a USD 300 million joint venture investment fund with the NFL to invest at the crossover of sports and digital
- There are currently 5 NFL owners who are also investor-owners in MLS: Robert Kraft, Clark Hunt, Paul Allen, Stan Kroenke and Arthur Blank (soon to be added is the Wilf family, owners of the NFL Minnesota Vikings, who will be minority owners of the new MLS Nashville franchise)
- The two attendance leaders in MLS, Seattle at 42,000 per game and Atlanta at 46,000 per game, both play in NFL stadia
- U.S. Soccer's policy with respect to USMNT and USWNT players kneeling during the

national anthem reflects the views of the NFL at least as much as MLS's investor-owners

4.7 The NFL's Challenge

An analysis of the U.S. Soccer-MLS/SUM-NFL relationship is important, not simply for historical reasons that carry over to the present, but because of the challenges that the NFL is currently facing.

Concussions in the NFL are a serious issue. The Frontline documentary *A League in Denial*, which is based on the book with the same title, is a devastating critique of the life-long damage American football can cause.

The litigation (which settled) between the NFL players and the league, belies the fact that additional concussion-based lawsuits as well as lawsuits focused on other aspects of the NFL's relationship to its players, are in preparation.

Concussion lawsuits have now been filed at the level of the NCAA and in youth American Football (Pop Warner) and as already mentioned in the context of the NCAA, the entire Ivy League now bars contact in American football practices (full contact will only occur on game day).

There is a distinct probability that the problem of concussions will not go away.

The question that no one can answer is -- how will this affect the NFL product and its revenue streams over the short, medium and long-term?

In the context of concussion litigation, there are arguably only two outcomes:

Either (1) the NFL does not make any fundamental rules changes (or makes only minor and ultimately non-impactful rules changes) and the game proceeds along as is,

Or (2) the NFL does make fundamental rules changes (to minimize or eliminate altogether concussions) and as a result the on-the-field product is necessarily altered and we have to assume dramatically so, if a meaningful impact on the concussion issue is to result.

Under scenario (1) the situation worsens from the standpoint of public perception, youth participation and litigation. In short, the settlement with the players will quickly evolve to be seen as a band-aid on an open wound that cannot heal.

Under scenario (2) the kind of fundamental rules changes needed would not only be an implied admission of guilt. A fundamental altering of the rules carries the strong possibility of a major impact on fan and corporate support and the overall monetization potential of the game.

Social media, mobile and all things digital in this context cuts in the direction of acceleration under both scenarios. Things will tend to happen sooner rather than later, and the NFL's reputation, brand and monetization potential (particularly corporate support) will deteriorate inevitably under either scenario. There is no palatable outcome.

4.8 Why Football is a Hedge and It's Potential Needs to be Unleashed

Football (being juxtaposed here with American football of the NFL variety) is a financial hedge for NFL owners. Why?

First, the NFL regular season is 16 games, with 8 home games. Today's crop of NFL stadia, which seat on average 60,000+ fans, are being used 8 times a year (if home field advantage is secured for the playoffs another 2 or 3 games could be added). The investment in such stadia, which easily surpasses USD 1 billion in construction costs per stadium carries a CAPEX burden. What can NFL owners do the other days of the year to generate stadium-based revenue (aside from concerts, dirt bike competitions, conventions, etc.)?

Clearly, one of the motivating factors in investing in MLS has to do with filling at least partially some of those empty dates and seats.

Let's share an important statistic. The MLS Seattle Sounders and the NFL Seattle Seahawks, who until fairly recently shared the same administrative staff and stadium (of the Seahawks), have less than 5% overlap in season ticket holders.

The same is true in Atlanta, where MLS's Atlanta United plays in the new Mercedes-Benz Stadium, home to the NFL Atlanta Falcons. There the season ticket overlap is 3%.

Given that the Sounders are drawing world-class attendance numbers at roughly 42,000 per game and Atlanta United is drawing approximately 46,000 (both at or above the Bundesliga average of 42,000), this is an important piece of information.

It means that there is a decent foundation for believing that football is not a cannibalizing threat to the NFL, at least from the standpoint of gate receipts. There are distinct fan bases involved. From a revenue generating perspective, the NFL's American football is fully or near being fully tapped, while football is largely untapped in terms of its revenue generating potential (from another perspective of course, that may be all the more reason to maintain the NFL's involvement -- which is exactly the idea being discussed).

Second, football in the United States and Canada is the only sport that can scale to world-class revenue, profit and ROI levels, using the European benchmarks of the EPL and Bundesliga in the short to medium term. The more quickly football arrives at that point, the greater and more meaningful the impact of the hedge.

Third, if the consequences of the concussion issue and debate continue, and every indication is that it will continue, the entire American football pipeline will be negatively affected. The NFL, the NCAA, high school and Pop Warner will all be dramatically impacted.

Physics is working against the NFL. 300-pound athletes capable of running the 40-yard dash in 4.5 seconds sets the stage for serious physical damage.

The bottom line is that all of this will inevitably lead to an impact on the all-important source of TV and corporate sponsorship revenues for the NFL.

Fourth, last and most importantly, football needs to be transformed. Instead of MLS serving as the lid on the pressure cooker of demand for football, MLS (or a rival to MLS) needs to adopt (a) a rebranding strategy, and (b) have its business model restructured to fully unlock football's potential. Both need to occur. Rebranding alone will not do it. Restructuring the business model alone will also not be enough. Only with both of these strategies working hand-in-hand will the revenue drivers of professional football be maximized.

Will football reach the heights of popularity, TV ratings and wealth creation of the NFL? The potential is clearly there. Without question football does have the potential to be bigger than the NHL, the NBA and possibly even baseball (in term of revenue not attendance). And that is the hedge. Football's scaling potential isn't simply domestic. It is international.

Couple these facts and arguments with the following assumption – namely, that the United States and Canada represent the only global venue today, that is capable of creating a world-class football league on a par with the EPL, Bundesliga, La Liga, etc. in the short to medium term (with all due respect to our friends in Brazil and China).

No investor group is better positioned to help football maximize its potential than the current crop of NFL owners (particularly those who have not yet invested in football).

Football is a hedge, not a threat to American football. It is a way out exactly when the NFL needs it the most.

Having the NFL fully cooperate, or at least having the current NFL owners in MLS fully cooperate, with an expedited MLS transition to a world-class football league, using the EPL and Bundesliga as benchmarks, is the best hedge the NFL owners have for their future.

Obviously, today this is not how the NFL and MLS owners and U.S. Soccer-MLS/SUM administrators see things.

The other hedge would be to create a rival league to MLS.

[1] Source: statista and the NFLPA.

[2] How each stadia is financed is an important issue, given the predominance of public-private partnership structures and the usual dependence on some form of municipality-linked revenue bond financing.

CHAPTER 5: MAJOR LEAGUE SOCCER (MLS): THE LID ON THE PRESSURE COOKER OF DEMAND FOR FOOTBALL

"It's a very hard league to play in. It's very physical, there's a lot of running. So there is a lot of physical work and to me, in my mind, too little play. . . What I'm talking about is actually a system or culture. I don't mean that the level of technical skills are low. I just mean there is a cultural void that needs to be filled."

--- Andrea Pirlo on MLS

"Playing football is very simple, but playing simple football is the hardest thing there is."

--- Johan Cruyff

"We all know that this league is just not like the Premier League or the Bundesliga and, of course, it can be frustrating on the pitch at times . . . If you compare it to Bayern Munich or the national team, the difference is huge, but I knew what I let myself in for."

--- Bastian Schweinsteiger on his Chicago Fire and MLS experience

"Instead of artificially inflating the expansion membership fees from an artificially scarce number of slots, the MLS should probably expand to at least 36 to 40 teams and merge with the NASL and USL to form a multitiered North American soccer pyramid. This is the only way to merge the internally and externally optimal league sizes, and to develop North

American soccer talent on a level to consistently play the beautiful game on par with the rest of the football world."

-- Professor John Vrooman

In any discussion about MLS, two things need to be done:

(1) deconstruct the mythology around MLS, clearly delineating what MLS is from what it is not, and

(2) place MLS in a global context, as the only legitimate lens for a critical analysis of its branding strategy, its business model and its future.

In Chapter 4 we discussed UEFA-FIFA's and the NFL's influence on U.S. Soccer-MLS/SUM. That is a permanent backdrop to any understanding of U.S. Soccer-MLS/SUM.

5.1 The Myth that MLS is a First Division Professional Football League

For the 2018 campaign the total salary burden for the 23 MLS teams with presumed 28-man rosters will be USD 200.3 million or USD 9.1 million per team [1]

Putting this in perspective, MLS's 2018 player payroll for 23 teams and roughly 650 players is approximately the same payroll as Manchester City's. One club's payroll in the EPL is the equivalent of the entire payroll of MLS.

We can slice and dice statistics all day long. MLS is not a first division league in comparison to any global football power. The first division leagues in the Big 5 European powers (the U.K., Germany, Spain, Italy and France), Brazil, Argentina, Mexico, etc. all maintain a standard of on-field excellence that dwarfs MLS.

In most of these countries the teams that comprise MLS would be hard pressed to maintain themselves in the second division and most would wind up in the third division.

The fact, if we are willing to face it, is that the USA does not have a legitimate first division league by any global standard.

This is one reason why discussions about promotion and relegation are more complicated than they seem. People are struggling to be promoted to a higher level of mediocrity.

The heated and hurried response from U.S. Soccer-MLS/SUM may be to cite attendance figures.

According to Soccer Stadium Digest (a publication sponsored by Populous, one of the leading public facilities architecture firms in the world), MLS averaged 22,106 for the 2017 season. MLS will inevitably compare that statistic to the NBA and the NHL (which both averaged around 17-18,000 per game for the 2016-17 campaign).

Both the NBA and NHL play indoors and if we really want to compare things, then we should ask what did those respective leagues generate in terms of revenue for 2016-17. The NBA generated USD 5 billion. The NHL around USD 4 billion.

We estimate that after 22 years in business, MLS is generating anywhere from a half billion to three-quarters of billion annually (in 2016 the Copa América Centenário produced a substantial one-off wind-fall) or a bit more than 1/10 the revenue of the NHL, and despite that MLS is still losing USD 100-150 million a year (a 22-year uninterrupted trend that shows no signs of abating).

But to compare apples to apples, MLS will say they outdrew established powers like Brazil (15,809 for their top-tier Campeonato Brasileiro) and Argentina (21,374 for the equivalent in Argentina). This is no time to explore the macro-economics of those two countries and how it has impacted the purchasing power of the local population, nor is this the place to analyze how Brazil and Argentina (among other non-European countries) are sending their best footballers to Europe in their pre-teen and teen years (nearly a four decades long trend), directly impacting the local football product which in turn impacts how Brazilian and Argentinian leisure time is spent.

What MLS does not tell you is that of the five revenue drivers of football, attendance is only one aspect of venues, and the other four revenue drivers, TV/digital, commercial, talent management and competitions are all underperforming when benchmarked against Europe generally and in particular when benchmarked against the global standard bearers, the EPL and the Bundesliga. For MLS the last two revenue drivers, talent management and competitions, provide marginal returns to MLS at best.

Applying the five revenue drivers of football forces MLS to do what it wants to avoid, namely, compare itself to the global standards of football excellence.

By that measure, MLS is in truth battling with the U.K. second division league, The Championship, and the second division Bundesliga, which by the way had respective average attendances of 20,119 and 21,735 in 2016-17.

To put the attendance idea in even better perspective, the EPL's average attendance figure for the 2016-17 campaign was 35,822 and the Bundesliga's 2016-17 campaign average attendance drew 41,511.

The average stadium size in the EPL is 38,519 and the average stadium size for the Bundesliga is 47,459. MLS's average stadium size for the 2018 campaign is 23,628 (or 21,978 if you discount that Seattle and Atlanta play in NFL venues).

Below the radar screen of the mainstream media, there is a debate raging in the football world in the USA and Canada. At the center of the debate are U.S. Soccer-

MLS/SUM and the rank and file football supporters across the USA and Canada. The hot topic of that debate is the question of promotion and relegation (Pro/Rel).

U.S. Soccer-MLS/SUM represent the status quo and are resistant to change, maintaining a public position that is categorically opposed to Pro/Rel.

The majority of the rank and file football supporters across the USA and Canada support Pro/Rel, albeit the actual implementation of Pro/Rel given the current restrictions of the football pyramid in the USA, is far from clear.

Before we deal with Pro/Rel and a number of other topics related to the professional game, a quick overview of MLS is warranted.

In our overview of MLS some information previously mentioned may be repeated. Please feel free to speed read through those paragraphs or skip them.

5.2 MLS Overview

No discussion of MLS makes sense without a context (obviously, the overlapping monopolies discussed above, and the self-interested roles being played by U.S. Soccer-MLS/SUM, UEFA-FIFA and the NFL is a constant undercurrent and generally a determining factor in MLS's performance or lack thereof).

There are three overlapping contexts to consider.

The first context is the USA's domestic professional sports leagues (excluding for the moment the plethora of other entertainment options available).

We have already established that the Big 4 (the NFL, MLB, the NBA and the NHL) generate approximately USD 25 billion a year in revenue. And it is also established that those four leagues represent the global standard of excellence in their respective sports.

The second context is European and concerns the leading professional football leagues and clubs of Europe. Like their U.S. Big 4 counterparts, these Big 5 European leagues and clubs represent the global standard of excellence for football.

The third context is the rest of the world, particularly those nations that are feeding the best of their footballing talent to Europe.

To reiterate, we are working with a global standard of excellence for leagues (the EPL and the Bundesliga) and clubs (Real Madrid, Barcelona, Bayern München, Paris St. Germain, Manchester United, Manchester City, Liverpool, Chelsea, etc.).

These leagues and clubs have their detractors, but in terms of revenue generation, attendance and setting the global standard of excellence, both on the field and off, they have no peer.

MLS, as the designated first division men's league, is the standard bearer for professional football in the USA and Canada. MLS is also the symbol we hold out to the world and the yardstick of our progress.

However, when measured against domestic standards of excellence, using the Big 4 as benchmarks, or measured against international standards of excellence using the EPL and the Bundesliga, MLS comes up woefully short.

In fact, since 1968, and the founding of the first North American Soccer League (NASL), no league, men or women, has been able to unlock the conundrum of the revenue generating potential for football in North America.

MLS/SUM has had 22 straight years of losses. These losses, which have been publicly admitted by MLS, are in the range of USD 100-150MM a year. This is more than two decades of a long vicious cycle.

There are three sanctioned professional football leagues in the USA and Canada for 2018. In addition to MLS, there is the National Women's Soccer League (NWSL) and the United Soccer League (USL).

These three leagues operate independently with no Pro/Rel and represent 66 teams for the 2018 season (MLS: 23, NWSL: 10, USL: 33). The North American Soccer League (NASL) has officially called off their

2018 season (more on this below in Chapter 6: U.S. Soccer's War).

MLS's player payroll for 2017 was a little over USD 200 million according to the MLS Player's Union. With the addition of LAFC for the 2018 season that payroll should expand – let's assume an addition of USD 10 million, so that the total MLS player payroll for 2018 is USD 210 million. Assuming an MLS roster size of 28 players per team would yield 644 players for a 23-team league. The average MLS team payroll for 2018 would be USD 9,130,435.

Given MLS's 8-year TV contract (2015-2022) for USD 90 million/year (a common assumption is that 2/3 of that goes to MLS, while 1/3 goes to U.S. Soccer), coupled with its collective bargaining agreement (CBA) with the players for five years (see the paragraph above), and an average stadium size of 22-23,000+ across its current 23 team league, means that the next five years of MLS's underperformance and losses is practically guaranteed. That will be 27 straight years of losses.

What kind of business model is this?

5.3 The Myth of the Single Entity

Our first task is to understand how any legal entity can post annual losses consecutively for over two decades and still survive. Particularly given the fact that MLS has publicly admitted annual losses of USD 100-150 million.

The legal entity we are working with is a Delaware limited liability company (LLC). An LLC, assuming it is being treated as a partnership for tax purposes, operates as a "pass-through" mechanism for the investors in the LLC. That means that gains and losses are "passed through" the LLC and then upstreamed to the investors (who may be investing on an individual basis or via another legal vehicle) at tax time.

In addition, LLCs are managed based on a contract known as an Operating Agreement.

The Operating Agreement is what guides the day-to-day affairs of the business and it spells out the obligations of the investors as well as the management team responsible for the LLC's performance.

Anyone on the outside looking in is at a distinct disadvantage, because the governing documents and the tax filings of MLS/SUM and the investors are not publicly available.

We have been told repeatedly that MLS is a single entity. The truth is that MLS has divided its league operating cost obligations in one LLC called MLS, and has set up another LLC called Soccer United Marketing (SUM) to focus on the revenue related activities of the league and any other complementary revenues arising out of the business.

All investor groups (23 for the 2018 season) in the MLS LLC are assumed to be investors in the SUM LLC (we will ignore Providence Equity's role in SUM for the time being and return to it shortly), and we also assume that all 23 investor groups share in the gains and losses pro rata.

Clearly, there has to be a division between what (i) MLS is responsible for, what (ii) SUM is responsible for, and what (iii) the investor-owners and their teams are responsible for.

When Don Garber says that MLS is losing USD 150 million a year does he mean that the MLS LLC is responsible for those losses? Or does he mean that the MLS LLC and the SUM LLC combined are responsible for those losses?

Whatever his response and based on our assumptions about LLCs as "pass through" mechanisms, we would have to assume that those losses have been upstreamed to the investors above both LLCs and are being allocated 1/23 to each investor.

When people say, therefore, that MLS is a single entity, the response is – it is and it isn't. MLS the league is clearly one LLC. But SUM plays a key role as a separate LLC in the overall scheme of things. We just don't know the full details.

First, we have no idea what SUM's cash flows are and what cash flow obligations exist. For instance, are all revenues that SUM generates obligatorily divided upstream pro rata amongst the 23 owners or are they used to off-set MLS's expenses? Or does SUM hold the prerogative of reinvesting those revenues and ignoring MLS's liabilities?

Second, MLS itself (ignoring SUM for the moment) is an umbrella organization for all 23 of the teams each of which technically exists as part of that LLC (the teams are not separate legal entities). Investor-owners in effect have a license from MLS to operate in a given geography of the country.

What I have been able to find to date is this:

At the team level and on the revenue side, investor-owners take 70% of ticket sales from home games and 100% of the following: local TV/broadcast, local sponsorships, other stadium revenue, team and youth academies.

At the team level on the expense side, investor-owners are responsible for 100% of: G&A (plus insurance for local operations), local marketing, stadium lease and operations, team staff, team travel, international exhibition game costs, team and youth academies.

At the league level on the revenue side, MLS retains 30% of local ticket sales and 100% of the following: national TV/broadcast, national sponsorships, national licensing and merchandising, ancillary properties and events, player sales/loans, expansion franchise fees, sales of percentage stakes in SUM.

At the league level on the expense side, MLS is responsible for 100% of: player acquisition and compensation, game costs, league offices, league marketing, league insurance, expansion franchise research and support.

In addition, stadium CAPEX and Beckham Rule player obligations are also part of team level expenses, that is, MLS has no obligation to cover those costs.

Why would MLS divide its business between two legal vehicles?

5.4 MLS's Business Model Inside Out

If MLS has losses of USD 150 million per year (these numbers have been subsequently corroborated by MLS officials), then we know that with 23 investors USD 6.52 million in average tax losses are being generated annually for each of the 23 MLS investor-owners.

The owners can certainly utilize those tax losses at their respective business ventures above the LLCs. These same investors could do the same thing with gains. They will each individually allocate those gains and losses as they see fit given the other enterprises and tax consequences in their portfolios. All of this, the decision-making process regarding gains and losses, takes place above both the MLS LLC and the SUM LLC.

Which brings us to a conclusion: from a tax perspective and on an annual operating basis, MLS as an investment is a wash for the investor-owners.

They can march into the sunset under the current scheme and that is exactly what they are doing.

In short, there is no financial incentive to change. And worse, no financial incentive to generate, much less maximize revenue. In fact, there may even be an incentive to limit revenue growth so as not to jeopardize the creation and flow of tax losses.

Put another way, the IRS Code allows for a LLC (i.e., MLS) to survive literally for decades if it can upstream losses.

If for any reason MLS/SUM has a cash short-fall, they can issue a capital call to investor-owners, sell a piece of SUM or wait for the next franchise fee distribution.

Given that many of MLS's investors are billionaires, each of them can find innumerable legal vehicles and ways to reduce taxable income in other business units by simply upstreaming the tax losses and allocating those losses against other business interests.

Given MLS's 22-year performance, if this occurred in any other industry vertical, it would be time to fire the management team, replace them and restructure the company and/or sell off the assets.

This is what happens when the football administrators for the USA and Canada do not have football as their #1 priority. Their priority is protecting the vested interests of the UEFA-FIFA and the NFL cartels.

Growing revenues to compete on a par with the EPL and Bundesliga is not part of MLS's game plan.

The so-called single entity is there to tread the financial waters not grow the business. With a salary cap of USD 4.035 million per team for 2018, you now have a better picture of how this league sustains itself and how it can do so indefinitely.

There is another myth about MLS that needs debunking. Namely, that MLS is "in it for the money" and that greed and revenues are driving the policy decisions at MLS and U.S. Soccer (on MLS's behalf).

Nothing could be further from the truth. Of the Big 4, the NHL is closest to MLS in terms of revenue generation. The NHL generated roughly USD 4 billion in revenues for the 2016-17 season. Despite the publicly admitted annual losses at MLS of USD 100-150 million, the revenues at MLS/SUM appear to be somewhere in the neighborhood of 1/10 (or slightly more) of the NHL's annual revenues. Let's assume USD 500 million annually.

The Bundesliga (I and II) generated collectively more than USD 3.5 billion in revenue for the 2016-17 campaign. The EPL generated over USD 5 billion revenue.

The only conclusion that makes sense is that MLS has a business model that "contains" wealth. By that I mean that despite having billionaire investors and triple digit millionaire investors, these deep pockets are not having an impact on the generation of revenue for MLS. MLS's very structure limits or "contains" the owner-investors wealth to such an extent that it cannot be expressed. The best example is the salary cap reference above.

In addition, of the five revenue drivers of football, the overwhelmingly dominant revenue category for MLS is gate receipts (one aspect of venues). TV and commercial revenue (two hugely important categories in European football) are practically an embarrassment – MLS's exiting TV contract is USD 90 million per year with approximately 1/3 of that amount going to the U.S. Soccer. That leaves USD 60 million annually to divide between 23 teams. The EPL's TV deal is the equivalent of USD 2.7 billion a year or over 27x MLS's deal (using the USD 60 million that goes to MLS, gives us a multiple of 45x over MLS's deal).

MLS's commercial revenue (licensing & merchandising and corporate sponsorships) is similarly and dramatically underperforming when compared to the top flight leagues and clubs of Europe.

The other two key categories of revenue, namely talent (i.e., player sales/acquisitions) and competitions (in Europe this means the lucrative UEFA championships) don't exist as meaningful revenue generators for MLS.

The investor-owners in MLS have the money to invest but the MLS business model doesn't allow them to make sufficient investment to generate anywhere near world-class revenues to take the league to the highest global standards of excellence and performance.

In addition, in the Big 4 each owner controls his or her team in a separate legal vehicle under that owner's control. That means 123 individual legal vehicles in addition of the legal vehicles that represent the respective leagues themselves.

Those leagues can in turn have any number of subsidiaries. For instance, Major League Baseball created MLB Advanced Media or MLBAM, the digital arm of MLB, which is owned by all of MLB's owners on a pro rata basis, meaning each owner has a 1/30 share. In 2017, MLBAM brought in more than USD 1 billion from digital revenue alone, that in theory was divided amongst the owners 1/30 each.

The fact that MLS is only one legal vehicle (ignoring SUM for the moment), in and through which all investors participate, means that each of the current 23 individual investors does not control its own separate legal vehicle. The upshot of this is that the Commissioner of MLS has disproportionate clout, responsibility and decision-making power, when compared to his counterpart Commissioners in the Big 4. And the corollary is also true, namely that the investor-owners in MLS have considerably less flexibility and responsibility when it comes to managing the value of their franchise. MLS's financial pot is much smaller than any of the Big 4, and the ability to manage day-to-day from the investor-owner's perspective has largely been delegated to the Commissioner and his staff. Value creation (or the lack thereof) is much more centralized.

5.5 The Klinsmann - Garber Debate

Even though Jürgen Klinsmann was fired in November 2016 his tenure carries symbolic importance.

Klinsmann stood for a fundamental principle of football excellence using the best national team, league and club benchmarks.

The football debate in the USA is about excellence versus mediocrity.

When Klinsmann was hired by Sunil Gulati he was hired as both USMNT manager and as technical director, which means that he had responsibility for preparing the USMNT for international and World Cup competitions but also for putting the football pyramid in order.

Klinsmann was a product of the German system. That system of talent discovery is a nationwide youth football program that is fully integrated from the grassroots local level to the professional level.

In conferring not only USMNT coaching duties but also technical director duties on Klinsmann, Sunil Gulati was attempting to bring the complete solution to the USA. It was an attempt to import the global standard of excellence and have it applied to the entire football pyramid in the USA below the professional level.

The assumption today is that because Klinsmann is no longer USMNT manager, the debate about excellence and mediocrity is over. Nothing could be further from the truth.

The real question is why did Sunil Gulati hire Jürgen Klinsmann in the first place? What was the strategy?

Of all the decisions that Sunil Gulati made as President of U.S. Soccer, the hiring of Jürgen Klinsmann was the boldest and in theory, the step that could have substantively changed things at the bottom of the pyramid (below the professional ranks) in the USA.

It was a recognition that youth football was the key to the USA's future, and by putting Klinsmann in place as technical director, Gulati thought he could bring his experience from Germany not only as a player and national team coach, but also as a player who rose from

180

grassroots German youth leagues to the professional ranks. Again in theory, and at the time, Klinsmann would bring the Bundesliga model to the USA.

The Klinsmann-Garber debate was and still is about the global standard of excellence versus mediocrity.

The Klinsmann experiment didn't work. What no one discusses, is that Klinsmann's presence was a symbolic challenge to Don Garber's authority. It was the closest that the USA has come to a full-fledged embodiment of the global excellence versus mediocrity debate.

While Gulati and Garber have always maintained a civil public tone when referring to one another, you can believe that Gulati was blamed by Don Garber behind the scenes for the Klinsmann-Garber disagreement.

When Klinsmann publicly declared and encouraged his players to choose Europe (the global standard of football excellence) over the United States and implicitly, over MLS, it was because in his opinion only by being exposed day-in day-out to the world's best competition, could the players on the USMNT become truly world-class, and ultimately, challenge for global respectability according to the highest global standards of the game, both on the pitch and off.

Klinsmann's statements were countered publicly by MLS Commissioner Don Garber. Don Garber's response was just shy of asking for Jürgen Klinsmann's head, but the debate was and still is about excellence versus mediocrity.

In the USA today, and across the entire football pyramid, from the lowest rungs of youth football to the professional ranks and national team play, the global standard of excellence in the USA has only one point of reference: the USWNT.

Jürgen Klinsmann, whatever his faults, was a legitimate reference point and a global standard of football excellence.

Looking back on his tenure, the pressure that Klinsmann was under is ironic.

We expected him as the USMNT's coach to deliver world-class results without having a team of world-class players.

What standard of excellence are we holding MLS to? Why we held Klinsmann to a higher standard of excellence than Don Garber is anybody's guess.

In a very real sense, Klinsmann's problem at the national team level, was and is directly related to Don Garber's and MLS's underperformance. And maybe, just maybe that is why Don Garber reacted with such vehemence to Klinsmann's statements. Because indirectly, Klinsmann was saying, whether we wanted to hear him or not, that MLS is not world-class and has no prospect of becoming world-class any time soon -- certainly not within the next decade.

People wanted Klinsmann to perform miracles. For Don Garber everyone is perfectly content with his strategy of slow and steady growth. In fact, slow and steady growth is a misnomer. MLS's growth strategy has at its essence another agenda, namely, maintaining the status quo.

Maintaining the status quo for MLS, means securing its place as the top professional league in the USA and Canada, irrespective of whether it is in reality a second or third tier league when compared against the global benchmarks.

In any valid analysis, MLS must be constantly compared against the global standards of excellence for this sport -- and right now that means Europe.

When compared to Europe, particularly at the league level with the EPL and Bundesliga, and at the club level with Real Madrid, Barcelona, Bayern Münich, Manchester City, Manchester United, Chelsea, Paris St. Germain, etc., MLS is losing ground, not gaining it.

In fact, MLS has lost ground over the past two decades not gained it.

MLS has established its own myth to the contrary, and that myth has been sold to the press and to the public extremely well.

The European leagues since MLS's inception in 1996, have outgrown, outspent and created an increasingly better product. The gap with Europe widened from 1996 until now, and promises to widen further.

The essence of the irony is that Don Garber gets consistent pats on the back for a job well-done, while the very product he has created and manages is the exact problem that Klinsmann had to face every day -- we are not producing world-class male football talent in the USA. It is just that simple.

Klinsmann, even as technical director, could not correct the wrongs at the top. And it is the top that dictates what happens at the bottom. The inspiration from pro sports leagues and the wish for dollars always trickles down. We all know this.

The NFL, the NBA, the WNBA, MLB and the NHL, hold the keys to providing young athletes with the incentive to aspire to greatness and the global standard of excellence. Not to mention the money. Each of those leagues is the global standard of excellence in its respective sport.

The best athletes in the USA groom themselves for years to reach that professional league standard of excellence. Until the top of the football pyramid, currently occupied by MLS, mirrors that same global standard of excellence, our best athletes and the money will not flow, either up or down the football pyramid.

5.6 MLS and the Vacuum at the Top

Strong arguments can be made that the off-balance sheet expenditures for Beckham Rule players would be better applied to our youth, and particularly to eliminating the Pay-to-Play model or at least eliminating the Pay-to-Play model for those who can't afford it (for the cynics who say that it is all Pay-to-Play regardless, because someone or some entity is paying, let's stop using that argument to ignore the problem of bringing the game to the millions who are excluded).

Let's look at other key metrics, that clearly indicate that the MLS strategy of maintaining the status quo and institutionalizing mediocrity, is undermining not only the USMNT but the entire football pyramid.

What is wrong with the men's game? The answer is simple. We do not have a men's league in the USA and Canada that can compete with the best leagues in Europe (or Latin America) day-in, day-out.

That is the problem. It was not Jürgen Klinsmann or any subsequent USMNT manager.

Even taking into account the competition of the Big 4 (the NFL, the NBA, MLB and the NHL), the NCAA, NASCAR, and dozens of other entertainment options that compete with live sports, MLS and professional football generally are underperforming, and dramatically so, across the five key revenue drivers of football: (1) venues, (2) TV, (3) commercial, (4) talent and (5) competitions.

These circumstances force us to face a brutal fact:

MLS cannot and will not get us to parity with the EPL and Bundesliga (as global benchmarks) under its current managerial regime and with its current business model and branding strategy.

As a nation, we are locked into a mediocre product. If MLS has its way, this prison of mediocrity will be with us for at least the next decade, and possibly beyond.

If we rely on the three main revenue drivers of professional football, venues, TV and commercial, it is clear that MLS has placed a severe revenue cap on its own future.

Don Garber's goal of expansion to 28 teams (with 32 teams likely) is simple to understand. The only meaningful revenue source that Don Garber has today are expansion fees (SUM is likely pulling down some revenues from the International Challenge Cup every summer and revenues will roll-in if the USA-Canada-Mexico bid for the WC 2026 comes to pass).

Closing the door at 28 teams means that Don Garber and MLS would be publicly shooting themselves in the foot. All other revenue streams are capped or virtually non-existent.

Its monopoly status and league expansion keeps up the ruse that MLS is improving financially. Nothing could be further from the truth.

MLS's current investors are impressive by any global standard. We have to assume that they are also extremely busy. Because if the owners took a closer look they could not help but see that MLS is an underperforming asset.

But is MLS an underperforming asset? Particularly, when new franchise entry fees are in the USD 150 million range? Isn't increasing franchise value the name of the game? If so, then the argument goes, Don Garber and MLS are doing a good job. Possibly even a very good job.

This MLS illusion is best captured in official statements from Commissioner Garber, that MLS will be one of the best leagues in the world by 2022.

Global status and football dominance all boils down to revenue.

In 2015-16, the NFL generated revenues of USD 12 billion, Major League Baseball came in at USD 8 billion, and for 2015-16 the NBA was at USD 5 billion and the NHL at USD 4 billion.

In 2013-14, the EPL generated revenues, which were the equivalent of USD 4 billion, while the Bundesliga generated the equivalent of USD 2.6 billion.

For hypothetical purposes let us assume that MLS generated USD 500 million in revenues in 2015.

If we assume 5 percent growth in revenues across the cited leagues until 2022, it means that in 2022 the NFL would generate revenues of USD 16.1 billion, Major League Baseball would generate 10.7 billion, the NBA 6.7 billion, the NHL 5.4 billion, the EPL 5.9 billion and the Bundesliga 3.9 billion.

Assuming the same rate of growth over the same period for MLS, would bring MLS to 670 million in revenues by 2022.

Two things are apparent. First, applying the same growth rate means the gap between MLS and the other leagues doesn't close over that time period (or any time period).

Second, unless MLS has a higher growth rate than the other leagues, the gap will stay the same, or in a worst-case scenario widen further.

Put another way, and using the EPL and Bundesliga as benchmarks, without a change in its business model and branding strategy, MLS's professed goal of being amongst the world's great football leagues will not happen.

Under the scenario outlined above, for MLS to bring itself to par with the Bundesliga by 2022, it would have to grow not 5 percent over that period, but greater than

40% a year, to arrive at the projected target of USD 3.9 billion.

There is absolutely nothing to indicate that MLS is ready to make the changes that would put professional football on a different footing to generate that kind of revenue and growth.

We haven't even discussed the business plan implications and pressure that 40+ percent compound growth for several consecutive years entails. It is clear that MLS's leadership believes strongly in its current business strategy and is content with its current plans and the status quo.

Part of the status quo means not having to worry about 40% percent growth rates.

Maintaining the status quo is MLS's goal. The status quo is being the premier football product offering for the USA and Canada while ignoring the global standard of excellence.

If someone were to ask MLS officials what they mean by MLS being amongst the best leagues in the world by 2022, that is, based on what criteria, they would be hard pressed to answer. If they say attendance, then most assuredly MLS will be drawing considerably less than our English and German first division benchmarks.

If they mention any of the other 5 revenue drivers of football, European benchmarks will again dwarf MLS.

MLS is the lid on the pressure cooker of demand for the sport in the USA and Canada. MLS's goal is a specific and strategic kind of growth - namely, growth to maintain occupancy of the top professional space in the USA and Canada. That is all. No more and no less.

The rank and file of football supporters, the people who are in the field, who are the heart and soul of this sport, who stretch their pocketbooks daily to support youth soccer, who pack up the kids and drive long distances are being ignored.

The kids themselves do not have a global standard of excellence to aspire to. Worse, they are being taken for granted. The rank and file votes have been diluted inside U.S. Soccer. Their influence has been marginalized.

The grassroots supporters of this sport, both suburban and urban, deserve better.

No business plan exists at MLS (much less at U.S. Soccer) to unleash the sport's full potential in the USA and Canada.

MLS has no interest in revenue maximization.

More importantly, MLS has every interest in making sure that no one else is able to maximize the revenue for professional football in the USA and Canada. That includes other leagues or investor groups that want to maximize revenue and promote a world-class professional model.

It will take a critical mass of MLS owners to change the league, and logically and logistically, that critical mass will only come together, when there is a consensus amongst the owners on the new route to be taken. Today for the owners, how to migrate from mediocrity to become the global standard of excellence is not clear.

Arriving at such a consensus will be difficult, if not impossible. Not only because each owner has all-consuming multiple responsibilities outside the league, but because the complexity of changing course involves a question of planning, execution, leadership and most of all vision. Such change cannot be expected to originate at MLS.

In this context, without a viable professional football league alternative to MLS, football fans have their hands tied. U.S. Soccer is not an independent body pushing the envelope on behalf of football fans everywhere. It's judgment and policies have been compromised. U.S. Soccer responds to higher authorities.

Practically and politically speaking, even with a viable challenger to MLS, there is no guarantee that U.S. Soccer would support a competitor. The pressure and control that MLS has at U.S. Soccer (and the pressure the NFL can exert through MLS) makes introducing the global standard of excellence through traditional channels, a near impossibility.

The only other alternative is if the entire pyramid below the professional ranks, takes a stand in favor of the global standard of excellence.

There are no examples of investor-owners in MLS, where the investor-owner has placed his heart and soul in the team and pulls out every stop to maximize that team's revenue and its success on the field and off, on a full-time basis.

In fact, MLS's single entity structure is there to thwart the possibility of MLS's own version of a maverick owner.

One owner (or ownership group) will not be able to turn around the Queen Mary that is MLS. Multiple owners might be able to dictate another story, another approach. But again, the odds of that happening, of achieving a consensus on a vision for change is very low.

Bucking the Commissioner is not going to happen at MLS.

What is possible is a grassroots football supporter's movement that originates below the professional level, brought together under the banner of the global standard of excellence.

A movement that empowers the fans to take control of their own football destiny from youth to the pros.

Until that happens, there will be a vacuum at the top for a professional football league in the USA and Canada, that matches or exceeds the global standards of excellence that the EPL and the Bundesliga represent.

5.7 Why Don Garber Went to Zürich?

U.S. Soccer's concept of professional league divisions is a farce and a red herring, because it masks MLS's real agenda and intention.

MLS's real agenda and intention is simple: what today we call the lower professional divisions (i.e., Division II) will eventually become MLS's official minor leagues. Major League Baseball (MLB) and the NBA maintain exactly that structure, why not MLS? Or so the reasoning goes.

By creating scarcity with their imposed monopoly, MLS can remain mediocre when compared to the global standards of football excellence, and yet still occupy the privileged position of the top league in the USA and Canada, without in fact being a top-tier league by global standards. If that isn't a restraint on fair trade what is?

In fact, MLS does not want to be the best football league in the world, because their mandate is to avoid that at all cost.

The NFL, MLB, the NBA and the NHL represent the global standard of excellence for their respective sports. And that is exactly what MLS is structured, managed and politically positioned to avoid.

Don Garber went to Zürich for the FIFA elections in 2015, because he is the most powerful man in the sport in the USA (and Canada). He went because he needed to horse trade. But for what?

The 2026 World Cup? That would appear to be the logical and obvious bargaining chip. Especially given the election of Gianni Infantino. The positioning Sunil Gulati effectuated with the Prince Ali vote in the 1st round (the USA's candidate at that point in the election), with the promise of Infantino support in the 2nd round, created the impression that the USA delivered the win for Infantino.

The logical conclusion, given FIFA's history of doing business, is that there has to be a quid pro quo. But what was this something-for-something at the FIFA bargaining table between Gulati, Garber and Infantino?

It wasn't the World Cup in 2026. The USA is already positioned and the pressure from the U.S. Department of Justice (DOJ) is still with us and will be for some time. If for whatever reason, Qatar falters, the USA is also positioned.

Clearly after Infantino's election, neither Russia nor Qatar were being seriously reconsidered (unless the

DOJ or the Swiss authorities turn up some additional and truly powerful and irrefutable evidence of corruption).

No, the real reason Don Garber went to Zürich, was to do one thing and one thing only – to make it clear to Infantino, that Infantino's election and U.S. Soccer's support (along with the Prince Ali votes that U.S. Soccer lined up) were in exchange for Don Garber being able to maintain the status quo in the USA.

5.8 What Does Maintaining the Football Status Quo in the USA Mean?

It means that MLS controls U.S. Soccer and the entire pyramid for the sport from the top (the pros) to the bottom (youth), and it has the rubber stamp approval of FIFA.

It means that football in the USA (and Canada) remains fragmented, both at the professional level and at the youth level and all levels in between, which perfectly serves U.S. Soccer-MLS/SUM's game plan for the sport.

It means U.S. Soccer-MLS/SUM further consolidating their power, for instance, by winning the rights for the Copa América Centenário in 2016, after the DOJ forced Traffic Sports and its partners (respectively from Brazil and Argentina) to relinquish their event organization right's package.

It means that U.S. Soccer-MLS/SUM is positioning itself to be a promoter of the sport not only in the USA but in the Americas.

The Copa América tournament, again coordinated by U.S. Soccer-MLS/SUM in 2016, naturally fits in the mid-off year schedule between World Cups, and like the European Championships, has the potential to become a natural part of the football landscape in the Americas.

It means that the weighted voting structure at U.S. Soccer (which essentially disempowers grassroots youth soccer and simultaneously empowers MLS) continues to guarantee MLS's disproportionate power and control over the sport.

It means that the Yedlin case continues to be a symbol of U.S. Soccer's war on soccer itself, particularly given that solidarity payments are a FIFA requirement.

It means that the war on women continues with U.S. Soccer maintaining a position against the women in their equal-pay-for-equal-work filing with the U.S. Equal Employment Opportunity Commission.

It means that labor generally (the players, coaches and referees) will remain at a distinct low-wage disadvantage for years to come when compared to the global benchmarks.

It means that the war against the NASL continues, which is in essence the struggle for (and against, from

MLS's perspective) promotion and relegation as a cornerstone for the sport.

It means the mediocrity that MLS symbolizes becomes more entrenched.

It means that U.S. Soccer-MLS/SUM can continue to carry out their real mandate – to strategically limit the upside and revenue generating potential of the sport.

It means that European hegemony in football remains as is, because today only the USA is positioned to rebalance the global power structure of the sport in the short-term, and that rebalancing (which means not only CONCACAF but also CONMEBOL) has the potential to create an UEFA-like presence in the Americas (North and South).

It means that the fans in the USA and Canada may never have the league and the clubs they deserve – a league and clubs that compete on a par with the EPL, the Bundesliga, La Liga, Serie A and Ligue 1, Brazil, Argentina, etc. as global standard bearers of excellence.

Don Garber's mandate is not what you think it is. His mandate is not to take this sport to the highest global standard of excellence on the field and off. His mandate is to make sure that that does <u>not</u> happen. Don Garber is there to make sure that we do not have a world-class league to rival the EPL, the Bundesliga, La Liga, etc. in the USA (and Canada).

The question is whether Gianni Infantino will go along with this? Is this the deal he struck with Garber? Were Don Garber and Sunil Gulati explicit in their demands? Or did they craft their proposal in vague and looser terms? Does Gianni Infantino really understand what Garber and Gulati mean when they say that the USA's plan for the future of football must take into account the "American Nuance"?

5.9 What is the American Nuance?

As long as MLS controls U.S. Soccer, and make no mistake about that fact (the change to weighted voting inside U.S. Soccer was done strictly for that purpose), they will do everything in their power to limit football's upside potential in every aspect, making sure in the process that the fan base does not expand too much, and more importantly, that football does not monetize too much.

The American Nuance is maintaining the status quo of the current MLS paradigm: no promotion and relegation; a league that controls FIFA's governing body for the sport in the USA; a league whose principle revenue stream is gate receipts (with the other four revenue drivers of football lagging way behind our European benchmarks); a league ownership model that provides the ability to move your team to another city if you so wish; a salary cap considerably below the global standard for average player salaries in Europe and Latin America; average stadia size of approximately 22,000 (below the U.K. and German second divisions); a TV contract that reflects the league's embedded mediocrity; three independent professional leagues; a dysfunctional football pyramid from top to bottom; MLS with 20+ consecutive years of losses; a branding strategy borrowed from the Big 4 that has proven itself incapable of carving out marketshare and driving monetization; and a burning desire to convince others (particularly FIFA) that this is a great business model and the best thing for the sport.

What everyone needs to realize, and Gianni Infantino in particular, is that the concept of the American Nuance is Orwellian. It is pure unadulterated double talk.

The NFL, MLB, the NBA and the NHL all embody the classic case of the American Nuance for professional sports, because they are monopolies which nevertheless maintain the global standard of excellence in their respective leagues. MLS is different, because MLS has no intention whatsoever of becoming the best football league in the world.

The reason this book is being written, is exactly because MLS and by default, U.S. Soccer, want to convince FIFA and the world that the American Nuance is exactly MLS's game plan.

That like the NFL, MLB, the NBA and the NHL, MLS will eventually become the global standard of excellence for football. That is simply not true. It is a falsehood.

As has already been explained, MLS is the lid on the pressure cooker of demand for football in the USA and Canada. Don Garber's task and MLS's purpose, its *raison d'être*, is to maintain that lid in place.

5.10 How the DOJ's Investigation of FIFA Led to U.S. Soccer-MLS/SUM Copa América Centenário Profits

FIFA is currently under investigation for criminal activity. These investigations are being led by the U.S. Department of Justice (DOJ) and Swiss investigative authorities.

As a direct result of these investigations and only because of these investigations, FIFA has adopted a number of reforms. It ousted Josef "Sepp" Blatter from his FIFA leadership role in 2015 as part of those reforms, and is conducting its own investigations in-house.

At a recent FIFA Congress held in Bahrain (May 2017) those in-house investigations have been brought into question. Two of the most senior leaders of FIFA's in-house investigations were fired and replaced at that May reunion of FIFA members and officials.

While Gianni Infantino, FIFA's new president has confirmed this change as simply a natural evolution of the new FIFA, major issues abound about the appropriateness of the move and its political motivations, and a slow-down of the investigation process is inevitable, given the change in personnel.

Meanwhile, the DOJ continues to bring indictments. The DOJ's focus has been on criminal activity that occurred in the United States (for instance, the use of U.S. based bank accounts to pay bribes and launder money), by individuals and organizations in the United States and elsewhere in North and South America.

The DOJ is relying on U.S. federal legislation known as the Racketeer Influenced and Corrupt Organizations Act (RICO). RICO was enacted in 1970 by Section 901(a) of the Organized Crime Control Act, and its specific purpose was to provide tools to the federal government to deal with the Mafia, a notoriously difficult target to prosecute.

One of the key individuals indicted by the DOJ pursuant to RICO was Chuck Blazer, an American, and the former head of CONCACAF, who was also on the FIFA Executive Committee (the highest ranking body inside FIFA prior to the reforms to combat global corruption).

It is well known and established beyond a shadow of a doubt, that Mr. Blazer had extremely close ties to the leadership at both U.S. Soccer (FIFA's representative in the USA) and Major League Soccer (MLS).

Another individual indicted by the DOJ, was J. Hawilla, a Brazilian and the founder of Traffic, a Brazilian sports promotion organization. Traffic was also the founder of the second incarnation and current version of the North American Soccer League (NASL), and also the holder of the rights to the Copa América Centenário (2016) tournament, which took place in the United States.

The rights to the Copa América tournament were lost by Traffic in the course of its prosecution in U.S. federal court and subsequently secured by MLS via SUM. SUM's management of that mega-event generated profits.

Those profits allowed for MLS to take the following steps:

- A cash distribution which generated a surplus at U.S. Soccer of USD 150MM,
- A buy-out of Providence Equity's 25% stake (which was diluted over time to 20% due to MLS expansion) in SUM,
- An undisclosed cash payment to CONMEBOL, the ultimate rights holder to the Copa América tournament, and
- Secure a USD 425MM line of credit from J.P. Morgan and Bank of America

In short, all profits are being used to reinforce the status quo.

The USA is currently facing a half-century of uninterrupted losses at the professional football league and team level.

And yet the Copa América tournament generated profits clearly in the hundreds of millions of dollars (again, an event managed by SUM and its select group of partners), and MLS is garnering franchise fees for expansion of the league at a baseline of USD 150MM, plus another estimated USD 150MM minimum for the required stadium commitment.

This is the power of the U.S. Soccer-MLS/SUM monopoly. I will leave it to the reader's imagination to contemplate the potential profits from the U.S. Soccer-MLS/SUM-led USA-Canada-Mexico 2026 World Cup bid, which is also being managed by U.S. Soccer-MLS/SUM through a dedicated special purpose vehicle (SPV).

There is demand for world-class football tournaments that maintain the global standard of excellence.

There is also demand for world-class football in the USA and Canada at the league and club level.

We simply do not have the product to fill that space. Yet.

This book is about bringing that global standard of excellence to the USA in the form of a league and clubs that are member-owned and controlled by the fans.   That is the driving impetus for The Football Manifesto.

5.11   The Strange Case of Providence Equity Partners

Providence Equity Partners (PEP) is a leading private equity investor in the media space. PEP took a 25% stake in SUM in 2012 for a reported USD 150 million, giving SUM a value of USD 600 million.

In 2017, PEP exited its 20% stake in SUM (which had been diluted over time by MLS league expansion) for a reported USD 400 million, giving SUM a value of USD 2 billion. That is a 2.7x multiple and a capital gain over the 5-year holding period of USD 250 million, for roughly a 23-24% IRR.

Providence could have invested in MLS itself, but it chose not to. PEP avoided the responsibilities and risks of a franchise.

It would be safe to assume that PEP believed that it would get a better return on investment from SUM than from MLS itself. No doubt there is room here to question that analysis – for instance, we would have to compare the increase in franchise values across the league and compare those increases with the increase in value generated by SUM over that five-year period. At the least, PEP concluded that given its portfolio and investment philosophy, SUM was within their sweet spot for investing in a way that MLS itself was not (obviously, from the standpoint of liquidity and exiting, SUM was the way to go).

Let's add a few logs to the fire. Given MLS's 20+ year track record of losses (publicly admitted by MLS to be in the USD 100-150 million range per annum), SUM as a separate LLC and as MLS's revenue generating arm, would clearly be the better investment from a cash flow perspective. In this context, there could be an argument made that SUM was in fact more valuable than MLS itself.

If that is the case, that is, that SUM is more valuable than MLS itself, it would mean that the combined MLS/SUM must be valued at somewhere around or below USD 4 billion.

Putting a value on MLS alone is complicated because of a number of factors. First, a valuation of MLS is complicated by the off-balance sheet Beckham player expenditures, and second, an even more complicated analysis would have to be made about the hard assets of each MLS franchise, namely the stadium involved and how that stadium was financed and whether that stadium is in fact part and parcel of the MLS license itself (it appears not to be). Add in the analysis of each club in terms of the five revenue drivers of football and the intangible of good will regarding each team's brand

and the permutations get interesting. At the very least, the CAPEX for stadia for each MLS franchise is not a simple question (particularly given public-private partnerships of varying degrees of complexity across the league). Third, despite Forbes' MLS valuations over the years, there simply have not been a sufficient number of acquisitions of existing MLS franchises to rely on a comparables analysis. And fourth and last, given the assumption that each MLS investor-owner is also a pro rata investor-owner in SUM, an additional USD 87 million for each franchise could be added to the potential value of each team acquisition (SUM's USD 2 billion value divided by 23). Then you would have to do (media) market analysis – hypothetically, a franchise in the New York City metro region would have more value that a franchise in Salt Lake City.

In 2014, and by way of comparison, Alliance the German insurance company, invested in Bayern Münich. For an 8.33% stake it paid USD 150 million (110 million Euros) in February of 2014, valuing Bayern Münich at USD 1.8 billion.

According to Forbes, as of June of 2017, Bayern Münich was valued at USD 2.713 billion (2.5 billion Euros).

There is something to be said for one of the leading clubs in Europe, Bayern Münich, being valued at more than SUM, the revenue-generating arm of MLS.

One European club is valued more than the company responsible for monetizing football in the USA and Canada. SUM is a company operating with a virtual monopoly in the USA and Canada, two of the richest countries in the world.

Let us look at the PEP investment in SUM from another angle.

NYCFC was founded in 2013. Sheik Mansour, the owner of Manchester City partnered with the Yankee's ownership group (the Yankee hold a 20% minority stake) and paid an MLS franchise fee of USD 100 million according to reports.

In theory, the investors in MLS (which obviously include Sheik Mansour and the Yankees) are assuming the higher risk of investing in a franchise, and therefore, should be receiving a better return on investment (ROI), to compensate for the added risk, when compared to the investment made by Providence Equity.

But just the opposite appears to be happening.

Investors today in MLS are expected to commit (1) a down-payment in the form of a franchise fee (USD 150 million), and (2) a commitment to build a stadium in the designated city that will be home to the franchise. Let's assume that the stadium costs USD 10,000 per seat. So a 20,000 seat stadium will cost USD 200 million.

For NYCFC this meant a firm commitment to MLS from Sheik Mansour of USD 300 million. As a person who lived and worked in New York City for many years and who also worked for New York City government, I can attest to the likely fact that given land costs and the necessity of land improvements, and assuming a construction project on land somewhere in the Bronx, Brooklyn or Queens, USD 300 million is a low-ball all-in figure for construction costs (aside from the absurdity of building a 20,000 seat stadium in New York City which was our initial working assumption).

NYCFC intended to build a 25 to 30,000 seat stadium (still an absurdity in New York City), so that the all-in price of the NYCFC franchise could easily come to USD 500 million. Obviously, the Yankees provided a temporary solution for the stadium requirement issue, by adapting Yankee Stadium for NYCFC.

By almost any measure, this initial outlay for NYCFC, is considerably more than Sheik Mansour paid for Manchester City. Since the purchase of Manchester City, however, Sheik Mansour has invested over USD 1 billion in the club and its infrastructure (not to mention players). The point is that the club came with infrastructure. Man City had a stadium that sat over 45,000 and it had dedicated training facilities, in short, it had substantial real estate holdings.

All of this brings me to a point that is worth considering. Namely, how is MLS justifying USD 150 million franchise fees and at least that amount again with the stadium commitment added in?

Clearly, there is a lot we do not know. For instance, we do not know how the franchise fee is being paid (if at all). It may be broken up into installments. It may be allocable to off-set the stadium fee requirement. In any case, USD 300MM for an MLS franchise must be compared to football club purchases in Europe.

Not only that but non-football sport's team purchases in the USA are also worth comparing, given the investment parameters MLS is demanding.

To put all of this in perspective, Swansea City AFC (which was owned 100% by the fans at the time) sold 68% of itself in mid-2016 for 100 million pounds (or roughly USD 133.5 million dollars) with the supporter's trust maintaining a 21.1% stake. This valued Swansea City as a whole at 147 million pounds (USD 196 million).

Swansea City AFC plays in the EPL. It has its own stadium (capacity: 21,088), training facilities and fan base. This is almost an ideal comparison with MLS franchises, because most of them are also building stadia roughly the equivalent of the Swansea City stadium. The only difference is that MLS is not the EPL.

If the investors in Swansea City paid say USD 200 million for outright 100% control wouldn't that be a better deal than a greenfield investment in MLS for USD 300MM (the USD 150 million franchise fee plus another USD 150 million for the stadium)? The answer is a clear yes! Of course that assumes that Swansea City can maintain itself in the EPL and won't get relegated (even if they get relegated, there are parachute payments to consider, etc.).

Since 2012 of course MLS has continued to expand. My whole point here is that some things from an investment standpoint don't quite make sense – at least for me.

PEP's investment in MLS was obviously needed at the time (could MLS at the time have made a capital call to existing investor-owners and been rebuffed?). And the fact that PEP structured a USD 300 million joint venture fund with the NFL to invest at the crossroads of digital and sports may simply be a coincidence (Each NFL owner (32) invested USD 1 million with PEP putting up USD 250+ million).

It is, nevertheless, strange to see investors in MLS who are clearly investing more money than PEP, be exposed to more risk and less ROI than PEP. I am sure there are "n" number of ways to think through this (i.e., the growth of franchise values over time for instance and the growth of SUM's valuation over time, not to mention the SUM cash flows/revenues) and somehow come out with the conclusion that the investors in MLS have the best deal, but right now I am having difficulty seeing that (particularly when you compare MLS to what you get when you buy an existing football club in Europe's Big 5 – which by the way always means you are buying into a league with promotion and relegation).

At least this discussion leads us into the related discussion of MLS's expansion plans.

One last point, PEP is also an investor in Univision, one of MLS's partners in the league's latest TV deal.

5.12 MLS's Expansion Plans

When speaking about expansion, it is hard to ignore the NYCFC case, if only because Sheik Mansour is one of if not the wealthiest investor in MLS.

Based on a proposed investment of USD 500MM (a minimum all-in cost for an MLS franchise fully built in the Bronx, Queens or Brooklyn), the NYCFC investment will cost a slight bit less than the average value for an NHL franchise which is USD 505 million. The NHL generated USD 4 billion last year in revenue. What am I missing here?

Most importantly from the standpoint of comparables -- NYCFC will cost more than the purchase value of Manchester City, Borussia Dortmund, Olympique Lyonnais, Hamburg SV, AS Roma, Olympique Marseilles, Valencia and Napoli (all franchise values from Forbes), as well as Paris St. Germain, which is estimated to have cost the Qatar Investment Authority 100MM Euros (USD 162MM).

Aside from the question of investing a quarter to half a billion dollars or more in an MLS franchise (and how that compares to investing in European clubs in the Big 5 or how it compares to investing in the Big 4 in the USA), the real question is what is the future of MLS?

Today, I do not see a viable route to recoup the investment made in MLS (and by recoup I mean a ROI in the neighborhood of PEP's ROI). There may be a way, but I do not see it.

The reason for that is simple. The benchmarks set by the EPL and the Bundesliga are in the multiples of billions annually in revenue (the Bundesliga just broke the 3 billion Euro barrier last season).

When you look at MLS through the lens of the five revenue drivers of football clubs, MLS appears to have reached a cap or a ceiling on just how much revenue they can generate.

There also appears to be no plan on the horizon to ramp up revenue and growth so as to be in-line with the EPL and the Bundesliga over a reasonable period of time (5 years? 10 years?).

As a result, my conclusion is that MLS is hoodwinking its investor-owners. MLS is selling growth based on a business model that is structured exactly to limit growth. The monopoly status that MLS maintains is driving the value increase of franchises. That value increase is also due to the growth of market demand.

Nothing, literally nothing on MLS's business model side or the branding side of the revenue equation is driving the franchise value increase. In short, the value is not due to the performance of the MLS business model. The value creation is directly related to the monopoly position held by MLS/SUM and the IRS Code, which allows chronic losses to be off-set via tax losses that are upstreamed above the MLS and SUM LLCs.

The conclusion should be obvious. There was never an intention on the part of MLS's founders to compete with the EPL, the Bundesliga or any other top-tier professional football league globally on the basis of revenues.

The exact opposite was the original intent of MLS's founders. MLS was purposefully structured from its inception to not compete with the best football leagues on the planet. This intent has been baked into the very structure of MLS and has been extended to the structure and fabric of U.S. Soccer itself.

New investor-owners in MLS have simply bowed to the MLS business model without any legitimate or credible critique.

The only task left is to bend FIFA to MLS's will and intention.

MLS could expand to 32 teams. It may even incorporate USL (now at 33 teams) and have a formal second division as a minor league (for instance, USL gets rebranded as MLS II). MLS may even decide in the future to work with promotion and relegation with USL (MLS II)(imagine a 32-team second division), but it would have to be done in the context of maintaining the existing parameters of the MLS business model. In short, the MLS status quo of football dominance is maintained.

Given the current state of football in the USA, a current state created and maintained by MLS, I feel comfortable in saying that MLS will never become world-class when using the global standard of excellence at the league or club level.

5.13 MLS's Stadia – the Ultimate Cap on League and Club Value Creation

In order for the USA to become #1 in the world, we will have to create football clubs and football club infrastructure. That includes stadia, training facilities and facilities for the club itself.

Suffice it to say that there is nothing wrong with the current crop of MLS stadia. Except for one thing. Only two stadia in MLS can be considered Division I stadia – Seattle and Atlanta – and both of those stadia are principally NFL stadia. Remove those two stadia and the average stadium size in MLS falls below 22,000.

TV revenues which drive every other sport's revenue growth and bottom line will never materialize with stadia that size. Not to mention revenue from the venues themselves. These two revenue drivers in turn by being limited, will guarantee the underperformance of commercial revenue for the league and clubs.

Second and third division size stadia generate second and third division size revenue.

No one knows this better than MLS.

So while MLS must be commended for adding important infrastructure to the game, it must also be held accountable for not creating a business model that will allow for substantial scaling to compete with our league and club global benchmarks.

Having the equivalent of a Real Madrid (Santiago Bernabéu: 81,044), Barcelona (Camp Nou: 99,354), Bayern Münich (Allianz Arena: 69,901), Borrussia Dortmund (Signal Park: 81,359) or a Manchester United (Old Trafford: 74,994) in MLS is simply not going to happen.

Without football clubs like these, the USA is fooling itself if it thinks it stands a chance of becoming world-class, much less #1 in the world. The USA will need 6 to 12 clubs (minimum) like these to become world-class and #1.

5.14 MLS's Salary Caps and Beckham Rule Players

The MLS Salary Cap. The MLS Salary Cap began with the inception of the league in 1996. Then it was USD 1.6 million.

Based on the current Collective Bargaining Agreement (CBA) the salary cap is/was as follows: for 2015: USD 3,490,000; for 2016: USD 3,660,000; for 2017: USD 3,845,000; for 2018: USD 4,035,000 and for 2019: USD 4,240,000.

MLS's salary cap is *per team* (presuming a 28-man roster). Again, that is per team, not per player.

Manchester City's payroll is the equivalent of MLS's entire projected league payroll for 23 teams for 2018.

Clearly, a well-capitalized rival league, in it for the long haul, would be able to easily exceed the MLS salary cap of USD 4.035 million per team, and put a better product on the field. This in turn would directly impact television and other digital content driven platforms and channels.

MLS team salaries are roughly 3% of their benchmark European club counterparts.

That statistic will worsen over the 8-year life (2015-2022) of the MLS TV contract.

The Beckham Rule. MLS's Designated Player Rules (or Beckham Rules) were created to attract high priced aging stars to the league. The assumption was and still is, that "old stars" create value for the league, attract fans to the games, and importantly, add credibility to the league's stature globally.

The Beckham Rule works as an "off balance sheet" mechanism, in that the cost of the player is covered by the league up to the maximum salary limit (roughly USD 457,500 as of 2016) and the remainder above that amount is covered by the franchise owner.

There is also an "impact" designated player concept of more recent vintage, which allows for the league to support the salary up to a higher amount (we are estimating USD 1 million), and this latter approach appears to be applicable to promising younger talent.

When the Beckham Rule is combined with the MLS salary cap (and any Targeted Allocation Monies (TAM)), the league finds itself in a revenue generating straight-jacket. In part revenue depends on the quality of the on-field product.

The inability to generate world-class revenues creates a "vicious cycle" of below average on-field performance, which directly impacts the ability of the product to be showcased for higher fees on television, which in turn undermines the attraction of a "critical mass" of young stars, which in turn continues to undermine the product on the field.

Revenue is a chicken or an egg dilemma. You have to spend to create revenue. But MLS's spending strategy for 20+ straight years has been unable to break out of the dilemma and generate world-class revenues on a par with our European benchmarks. Lamentably, the new MLS TV contract does not change that dynamic. The chicken or egg dilemma remains.

A Monopoly Mentality. MLS's control of the first division space and the league's media exposure, despite at best mediocre ratings and a declining trend, coupled with income from expansion fees, new stadia and the eight-year television contract, reinforces the public perception that the league is pursuing a steady and healthy trajectory.

The mystery is why would the MLS investor-owners, either individually or collectively, after making substantial investments in the sport, in many cases in the hundreds of millions of dollars, settle for a strategy that does not maximize revenue.

SUM of course provides the ruse of revenue maximization, when in fact what SUM is doing is occupying the "soccer space" to the greatest extent possible while avoiding revenue maximization at all costs.

In this context, it is also unclear what role the investor-owners play in the overall issue of MLS governance.

A completely cynical view of the current MLS picture is that the league is being driven by a business model focused on generating tax losses. If that is true, then incentives in the IRS Code are the real driver of the business model and not maximizing revenue, much less profits.

In truth, the gains MLS is experiencing, if they can be characterized as such (increased attendance and new stadia cannot be denied), are due far more to the growing demand in the marketplace for football, than anything in MLS's business model or its branding strategy.

From another perspective, MLS is simply a placeholder league. It is occupying the top position in the professional league hierarchy for the sport, it faces no real threat and whatever plans it makes are largely part of a strategy to maintain the status quo.

Maintaining the status quo means keeping a lid on the explosive growth potential that professional football has in the United States and Canada.

MLS in its current incarnation is not only incapable of realizing that potential, it has every intention of avoiding that outcome.

[1] Source: MLSPU.

CHAPTER 6: U.S. SOCCER'S WAR

"In this day and age, it's about equality. It's about equal rights. It's about equal pay. We're pushing for that. We believe now the time is right because we believe it's our responsibility for women's sports and specifically for women's soccer to do whatever it takes to push for equal pay and equal rights. And to be treated with respect."

--- Hope Solo, former goalkeeper USWNT, World Cup and Olympic gold medal winner

"Frankly, the leadership of U.S. Soccer has failed all of its stakeholders: players, fans, sponsors and those of us who have invested in professional soccer. Getting back on track requires fundamental change in the structure and management of the sport in our country, starting with a change in the Federation's leadership".

--- Rocco Commisso, Owner, New York Cosmos

"It's not working for the underserved community. . . . It's working for the white kids. People don't want to talk about it."

--- Doug Andreassen, Chairman, U.S. Soccer's Diversity Task Force from an article published in The Guardian

U.S. Soccer is fighting wars on several fronts.

Against the North American Soccer League (NASL). NASL is suing U.S. Soccer in federal court in New York City's Eastern District, claiming that its decertification as a second division league has put its very survival in jeopardy. A motion for an immediate injunction to reverse that decision by U.S. Soccer has been denied, and a recent decision by the federal court of appeals sustained the findings of the lower court. Based on that appeal's court ruling NASL has officially called off its 2018 season. Nevertheless, the lawsuit proceeds.

NASL is also alleging that the professional divisions themselves along with their divisional requirements, are arbitrary, discriminatory and prejudicial to any non-first division league, and that behind this move U.S. Soccer is working with MLS to create anti-competitive and artificial barriers to enter the marketplace of professional football.

This is the same district court that is pursuing charges against a number of FIFA officials and their subordinates and partners pursuant to a global corruption scandal. A number of convictions, plea bargains, jail terms and fines have resulted and there appears to be no end in sight.

Against Lower Division Professional Clubs. Another U.S. Soccer war, involves two clubs from the lower divisions of the professional ranks, Miami FC (of the NASL) and the Kingston Stockade (of the fourth tier National Premier Soccer League) who have brought a claim to the Court of Arbitration for Sport in Lausanne, Switzerland, against U.S. Soccer, CONCACAF and FIFA, alleging that by not requiring promotion and relegation (Pro/Rel) in the United States, these regulatory bodies are in violation of FIFA's rules which mandate Pro/Rel.

Against youth football club programs. The Yedlin case, which is pending before FIFA's Dispute Resolution Chamber (DRC), has to do with a global and customary scheme according to FIFA's rules, of compensating the original youth club (that is the club where the player in question began his/her training) by forwarding a percentage of the acquisition payment from a professional club for that player's services. The reasoning here is that the professional club, which did not spend years preparing and training said player should allocate a small portion of its contract fees for the player to the original club as a form of incentive. This is a common practice globally. U.S. Soccer and MLS both claim that such practices violate U.S. anti-trust laws.

Against women having equal pay. Members of the USWNT have filed a wage discrimination lawsuit against U.S. Soccer. Winners of three World Cups and four Olympic gold medals, the USWNT has set the global standard of excellence for the sport in the USA and are the only global standard bearer of excellence we have.

No doubt there may be other grievances from other football stakeholders up and down the pyramid that have been missed here (please forgive me if that is the case – and write and let me know what is missing – no stone can remain unturned in this quest to reform football), but to synopsize, the above referenced litigation delineates three (3) overarching issues about which U.S. Soccer is resisting change:

(1) Promotion & Relegation

(2) Support of Youth Football

(3) Equal Pay for Women

6.1 Thoughts on Promotion & Relegation (Pro/Rel)

"Carlos [Cordeiro] will have this challenge . . . to bring in a football culture to the whole country . . . and the league system that exists in the United States with the closed league and so on there are many challenges that have to be tackled."
--- Gianni Infantino, FIFA President, in an ESPN interview the week after the U.S. Soccer elections on February 10, 2018

Peter Wilt, a long-time football administrator put together one of the most comprehensive thought-pieces on Pro/Rel in Howler Magazine in its Spring 2017 issue and it is available online.

Riccardo Silva, owner of Miami FC of the NASL commissioned a study on Pro/Rel by Deloitte and in the football blogosphere Pro/Rel is the hot topic of discussion. Mr. Silva and Dennis Crawley of the Kingston Stockade of the NPSL are appealing to the Court of Arbitration for Sport in Lausanne, Switzerland, alleging that U.S. Soccer and MLS are ignoring FIFA's mandate for Pro/Rel.

U.S. Soccer-MLS/SUM have made their position clear. They are definitively against Pro/Rel.

Their reasoning is largely based on the thesis that the investors in MLS/SUM assumed that they were investing in a monopoly, that is, a league that would not be subject to Pro/Rel and based on the amount of money that they have invested it would be unfair and quite possibly a contract violation to impose Pro/Rel on these investors.

Pro/Rel raises any number of issues. I want to narrow down the focus and touch a few buttons that in large measure are being ignored.

At least four of MLS's investors, Stan Kroenke, Erick Thohir, Dietrich Mateschitz and Sheik Mansour have investments in European football clubs and leagues – respectively, Arsenal, Inter Milan, RB Leipzig and Manchester City. No one is more exposed to Pro/Rel and the implications of it than they are (RB Leipzig rose from the German 5th division to the top of the Bundesliga).

As for these four investors with some knowledge, experience and exposure to the risks of Pro/Rel and the other MLS investors, there is the question of introducing Pro/Rel and have it prejudice their investment – in that being demoted to a second division league or below would entail a major disruption of their value creation proposition.

Why would Stan Kroenke, Erick Thohir, Dietrich Mateschitz and Sheik Mansour invest in clubs and leagues that have Pro/Rel? Because those leagues are in Europe and the value creation proposition is in the billions of Euros in annual revenue. The likelihood of their clubs being demoted is slim to nil. They spend too much payroll on talent for that to occur. Is there a risk, yes. But it is minimal. Meanwhile, they own clubs that are worth hundreds of millions if not billions of dollars/Euros.

MLS is not at all in that ballgame. And that is the strange part. Again, MLS's salary cap in 2018 is USD 4,035,000. That is per team. Not per player. In fact, that MLS salary cap is below the average player salary in the EPL.

So these MLS investors most of whom are extremely wealthy (triple digit millionaires and billionaires) are really not financially stretched by what they have to shell out at MLS. Here's why, and we have mentioned this already above.

MLS is an LLC, which means it is a pass-through mechanism. Gains and losses are literally passed through the LLC and upstreamed (we assume pro rata) to each individual investor (or his/her designated legal vehicle) and are treated for tax purposes accordingly, either as a gain or a loss.

I have already mentioned that it is this scheme, which depends entirely on the IRS Code, that has allowed MLS to survive for over two decades when it is losing anywhere from USD 100-150 million a year.

Pro/Rel doesn't work for MLS because it would mean bringing an "uninvited" third party from say USL (not originally part of the MLS brotherhood) into a scheme that has been tailored exclusively for them.

In large measure, the MLS business model has removed any and all incentive to maximize revenue. In fact, too much revenue could jeopardize the tax loss benefits.

There is another issue, however, that is more fascinating. What would a USL franchise be promoted to? MLS? What would such a club be gaining?

Sure we can argue that USL revenues are considerably below MLS's. But MLS's revenues are already so low as to be embarrassing when compared to the EPL, Bundesliga or any of the major European leagues. Pro/Rel in fact would elevate clubs into the same revenue straight-jacket that MLS is suffering from now.

MLS's main revenue source for clubs is gate receipts. TV and commercial are marginal. Would this make sense for say FC Cincinnati that is already generating decent gate? What else would they gain by being a part of MLS?

The reason U.S. Soccer and MLS/SUM are against Pro/Rel is that it would move strongly in the direction of deconstructing their entire business model. That in turn would expose MLS to non-MLS owners who were willing to spend considerably more than MLS is willing to pay to maintain their clubs in a so-called Division I league.

The absurdity of Pro/Rel in the USA is that there really is little money involved when compared to Europe. We do not have the equivalent of Real Madrid, Barcelona, Manchester City, Bayern Münich and PSG in the USA, much less a lucrative multi-billion a year TV contract to divide up.

Pro/Rel in the USA as a result is a fight for the crumbs falling off of MLS/SUM's table. Those crumbs are simply not that impressive.

Pro/Rel in this context is a distraction.

The challenge is to create a real Division I league in the USA that has clubs equivalent to Real Madrid, Barcelona, Man U, etc. That is the only focus worthy of our attention right now.

Peter Wilt lays out a number of permutations on how Pro/Rel could be introduced. The underlying assumption for all those permutations is the same – namely, that with Pro/Rel people will invest. The sky will be the limit.

Lamentably, without major changes in how this game is structured (i.e., league and club business models) at the professional level and without a major readjustment in how this game is branded, this sport will never yield the revenue of Europe. Pro/Rel alone will not solve this core problem.

Without those changes the USA will always be second tier at best, third tier in practice. And we haven't even dealt with the added but necessary burden of restructuring the pyramid below MLS (that youth player pipeline is crucial for the future of the sport – more important by a long-shot than MLS's next move).

For those who view MLS as a legitimate Division I league (it is not), there is an air of intimidation about MLS and what it stands for. In truth, despite the billionaire investors, MLS is not spending or earning that much annually. As we have said, yearly salaries for the entire league are a bit more than USD 200 million. Again, that is what Manchester City spends annually on player payroll.

The problem isn't MLS. The problem is a lack of vision about how to create the club equivalent of Real Madrid, Barcelona and PSG in the USA. And that has nothing to do with Pro/Rel.

Creating these clubs and a new league to support them should be the priority, not Pro/Rel. Create stability first.

The Football Manifesto's purpose is to create that league and those clubs in the USA.

We don't need MLS's permission to create that league or those clubs. We don't need U.S. Soccer's permission (U.S. Soccer is an approval mechanism after the fact). We don't need FIFA approval.

Once that league and those clubs are created then MLS will be demanding Pro/Rel.

The false assumption lurking in this debate is that by imposing Pro/Rel on the entire pyramid (or on a portion of it using one of Peter Wilt's permutations or some other permutation) it will be like Hans Brinker taking his finger out of the dyke.

A massive flood of interest in the sport is counter-productive without a structure in place to guide those financial forces. Right now we do not have that structure in place in the USA. U.S. Soccer-MLS/SUM is not here to play that role. No existing or proposed league structure below MLS fills that bill.

Pro/Rel must be thought of as one tool amongst other tools that need to be brought to bear on properly structuring football in the USA. The timing, structure and scope of Pro/Rel is just as important as the concept of Pro/Rel. Going about Pro/Rel in any other fashion is time and money spent in a war with U.S. Soccer-MLS/SUM that can only lead to partial solutions. Pro/Rel is at best a partial solution and at worst an invitation to chaos, in addition to the chaos that we are already dealing with.

There is one more issue regarding Pro/Rel worth raising. That is the millionaires versus billionaires issue. All of the professional leagues in the USA have minimum net worth requirements. This means that to become an owner you have to establish that you can afford to invest and maintain a league and clubs in that league. In short, even below MLS there is still a requirement that high net worth individuals (HNWIs) be the owners of teams in leagues. If you are in the top 1/10 of 1% of the wealthy in the USA you are welcomed with open arms to join the exclusive club of owners in a given professional football league.

There are egos and varying degrees of snobbery everywhere. The issue of not being wealthy enough to buy-in to MLS, means that you are not eligible to join "our club." It should, therefore, not be surprising that MLS, as virtually a private club that hand picks its members, should be against Pro/Rel.

For instance, Mr. Rocco Commisso, the owner of the Cosmos, is a wealthy individual, but he is not "our kind of wealthy individual" or so the reasoning appears to go with respect to Pro/Rel and admission to MLS (the Cosmos won the NASL championship several times and in a Pro/Rel scheme they would have automatically been elevated to play in MLS as the Division I league).

My point and the purpose of The Football Manifesto is to open the game, league and club idea to everyone – everyone below the top 1/10 of 1% of the wealthy, as well as everyone in that particular earnings bracket. Fans and communities should be able to be member-owners of the club they support irrespective of how much money they have or earn annually.

To drive this point home, Barcelona's more than 180,000 voting members generate more than USD 30 million in membership fees annually. That is six times (6x) the MLS salary cap per team. Their average annual individual membership fee is roughly USD 200.00 a year.

6.2 The Destabilizing Impact of Three Independent Pro Football Leagues

In addition to MLS, the United States and Canada have the women's Division I pro league the National Women's Soccer League (NWSL) and the Division II men's United Soccer League (USL). And all the while Canada is contemplating its own Division I men's league.

When comparing MLS, NWSL and USL, however, we are faced with a quandary. What does the status of Division I and Division II really mean?

Because there is no promotion or relegation involved between divisions, the three leagues are in essence three parallel professional leagues. The difference is in the amount of money involved and the respective business models.

If an investor or a group of investors decided to invest in USL and raise its standards both on and off the field, it could rival MLS almost overnight. Because the teams in USL are independent franchises (as opposed to MLS's single entity structure), they have (in theory) full liberty to spend as they see fit.

The question is whether those league's business models mimic the business models of the past 45 years, or whether they bring (or are planning to bring) a truly game changing approach to the marketplace.

To date the answer is clear. There is nothing that NWSL or USL is doing to position either league to be a rival to MLS.

The Football Manifesto is an invitation to football fans everywhere to take the current situation into our own hands and create the league and the clubs that this country deserves.

6.3 NASL

"The definition of insanity is doing the same thing over and over again, but expecting different results".
--- Albert Einstein

Former NASL Commissioner Bill Peterson, was quite open about his mandate. It was to transform NASL into the top professional football league in the USA and Canada and the direct rival to MLS.

Lamentably, it was never clear how NASL intended to achieve that goal.

The brands that NASL adopted were disproportionately "old school" and either harkened back to the original NASL (e.g., Cosmos, the Rowdies and Strikers, etc.) or new names were adopted using a nevertheless generic pattern of thinking for brand origination that borrowed heavily from the marketing and branding paradigm of the Big 4 (e.g., Indy Eleven, SF Deltas). [1]

On the business model side of the equation, NASL was just as unimaginative. It simply borrowed the same business model as the original NASL, which clearly did not work.

NASL never developed a short, medium and long-term strategy to maximize the 5 revenue drivers of football clubs.

That model allowed NASL team owners to manage their operating budgets with no parameters imposed (e.g., salary caps) resulting in a league business model of total flexibility (or abandon depending on your perspective) and minimal controls. One of the purposes of having a league is to standardize operations for the communal benefit of all franchises and the league itself, and having a strategy to allow the league to scale to world-class status (NASL's supposed primary objective).

When coupled with little or no strategy about how to go head-to-head against MLS in top-tier media markets and opting for secondary media markets for the initial set of franchises (initially and for most of their existence, the Cosmos had to play on Long Island and not in New York City) and then secondary and even tertiary media markets for expansion franchises (e.g., Puerto Rico), NASL was a ship without a compass.

As a group, the NASL owners were single-digit and double-digit millionaires as opposed to MLS's mix of triple digit millionaires and billionaires (there may be individual exceptions but as a group the NASL investors were/are much weaker financially than their brethren at MLS). The cities/regions in which NASL chose to install itself were noteworthy for avoiding direct market confrontation with MLS. The average stadium size of NASL teams was barely 5,000 and so it was no surprise to see that a meaningful nationwide TV contract was not forthcoming, much less significant revenue generating potential from the commercial side of the revenue equation.

NASL could never generate the revenue from the three most important revenue generators – venues, TV and commercial.

Then for the 2017 season, formerly Division III league, USL, upon application to U.S. Soccer, was elevated from Division III to Division II, directly competing with NASL nationwide.

A few years ago the argument for investing in NASL, if you believed the story of head-to-head competition with MLS, was to get into the game of professional football for a low entry fee (approximately USD 5 million, which might vary depending on the venue, versus MLS's USD 150 million entry fee), grow the business and wait for Pro/Rel to be imposed on the entire football pyramid, including MLS.

The two key underlying assumptions of such an investment in NASL were that:

(1) Pro/Rel from any rational standpoint was best for the game and would be adopted in a reasonable time frame, and

(2) U.S. Soccer as FIFA's representative in the USA was a neutral administrator of the game and therefore not subject to pressure from other competing professional leagues.

Both assumptions were misguided.

There are strong arguments to support the notion that NASL was a legitimate threat to MLS, but only because it was designated as a professional league. Not because of its Division II status.

In theory, a sanctioned professional league (regardless of divisional status) with a better branding strategy and business model, could pose a legitimate threat to MLS in a head-to-head confrontation.

The idea of creating an ABA-NBA-like rivalry or an AFL-NFL-like rivalry or WHA-NHL-like rivalry is not farfetched.

However, in each of those cases of rival leagues, all six leagues were struggling to become the global standard of excellence in their respective sports. The only reason the mergers took place was exactly because each of the incumbent leagues saw in their more innovative rivals a reason to work together via merger.

To date no legitimate rival to MLS has appeared. NASL never came close to filling that role. Given what we know about the NFL's influence in football, one has to wonder about Commissioner Peterson's (a former NFL employee) good faith in steering the NASL's path.

As has been discussed in our critique of MLS, the divisional status imposed on professional football leagues that is conferred by U.S. Soccer is based on a subjective set of criteria. The deliberation process used internally at U.S. Soccer to establish those criteria is clearly tainted, in that MLS Commissioner Don Garber is a key voting member of U.S. Soccer's professional leagues committee (Garber's influence goes considerably beyond voting, even if he does not vote). The conflict of interest, however, gets worse.

It gets worse because the very concept of professional league divisions is a red herring and a smoke screen for MLS's real agenda.

MLS's goal is to create a permanent unalterable structure of major and minor leagues in football that mirrors the professional league monopoly arrangements that Major League Baseball has with its minor leagues or that the NBA has with its D League. Neither the NFL nor the NHL have a minor league as a feeder mechanism, because the NCAA fulfills that role.

In fact, with a prohibition against Pro/Rel that is exactly what MLS has, a major league monopoly.

From one perspective MLS's public position as being categorically opposed to Pro/Rel is interesting because from a technical standpoint, it is not in MLS's purview to pronounce on that issue. Pro/Rel is an issue and represents a status to be conferred (or not) by U.S. Soccer, not MLS.

In the lawsuit that NASL brought in federal district court for the Eastern District in Brooklyn, part of its case rests on the false premise that Division II status is the life-blood of the league and that without that status it will go out of business.

NASL has missed a key point. Given its current branding strategy and business model, NASL will go out of business with or without Division II status. The only real life-blood that NASL could ask for, but will never get because it fails to meet the criteria, is Division I status (the fact that NWSL is a Division I league clearly indicates that U.S. Soccer is nothing less than arbitrary in the application of its league divisional criteria).

When coupled with U.S. Soccer's conferral of Division II status on USL, the only viable argument before the court (from NASL's perspective) would be a misapplication of Division II criteria with respect to NASL and USL. Importantly, USL is a 33-team Division II league (for 2018), of which 20 teams are affiliated with MLS teams (10 of the 20 are owned by MLS teams). The MLS-USL affiliation partnership idea should be enough for any federal court to give pause. What clearer restraint of trade could there be?

Was it reasonable to deny Division II status to NASL? Is that really the question here?

Isn't the real question whether U.S. Soccer and MLS/SUM are conspiring to establish the professional league divisional criteria as a distraction from their real agenda, which is to maintain (i) a monopoly at the Division I level, and (ii) its corollary to guarantee that no rival appears at the Division I level in the USA?

NASL, despite their ineptitude, was the only threat. USL has been "bought off" by MLS lock, stock and barrel.

The question is whether the court will see behind the ruse that U.S. Soccer and MLS/SUM have created. Even if the court sees behind the ruse and exposes it, there is no guarantee of a legal solution. Either because the claim and desired relief wasn't contained in the pleadings at all or was improperly pled. There is also the question of the relevant market.

Speculation about the legal outcome of NASL v. U.S. Soccer misses the point. NASL is in trouble regardless. NASL has already publicly announced the cancellation of the 2018 season.

If MLS truly represented the global standard of excellence, the case in Brooklyn would present a radically different fact pattern. In point of fact, there might not even be a lawsuit.

MLS does not represent that standard, and its *raison d'etre* is to avoid, block and undermine any and all third parties (globally) that embrace that global standard of excellence from entering the USA marketplace.

That is the restraint of trade and the anti-competitive practices that U.S. Soccer-MLS/SUM represent.

The handwriting for NASL's demise is on the wall.

Even if by some miracle NASL was to win its case against U.S. Soccer, its current branding strategy and business model (independent of any divisional designation) guarantees its failure as a business venture.

Some of NASL's franchises have already "moved" to USL (or NPSL) and now comprise soccer's minor leagues, a role that USL has wholeheartedly embraced. Another member (Minnesota) joined MLS for the 2017 season.

As MLS's expands, USL will expand, and eventually the financial "trickle down" to USL from U.S. Soccer-MLS/SUM will begin to occur.

Without Pro/Rel, the NASL valuation analysis, the actual justification to make an investment in NASL falls apart.

While laudable in principle, the idea that NASL owners are totally independent and can craft their own business model, has meant that they are largely copying the freedom and practices of the original NASL owners from the 1960s and 1970s, without nearly the same capital base.

NASL offered nothing new. The only meaningful change that impacts analytics is occurring outside of NASL and independent of it, namely the compelling demographic trends in the USA and Canada that support the sport of football.

From the standpoint of monetization, the problem is that NASL was simply unable to take advantage of those demographic changes and trends.

NASL as a league does not have a future, without some dramatic new ideas. Changing the branding strategy and business model is key, but nothing on the horizon indicates that NASL and its possible remaining owners are capable, much less interested in those kinds of adjustments.

When coupled with what can only be described as a strange expansion strategy, that was largely focused on secondary and tertiary media markets, the (former) owners in NASL (the few that are left) have to be wondering how they will ever achieve Division I status let alone recoup their investment, particularly given that they do not control U.S. Soccer's decision-making process, and MLS does.

As we have said, the assignment by U.S. Soccer of certain professional leagues to a given division is really a ruse. It appears to be a signal to FIFA that things are evolving toward Pro/Rel, when in fact nothing could be further from the truth.

The political and institutional squeeze is on and Don Garber's visit to Zürich was to make sure that neither the NASL, nor any other men's league with Division I aspirations, will ever see the light of day.

That is the American Nuance.

6.4 Youth Football's Dilemma

There are three (3) nationwide youth football organizations in the USA: U.S. Youth Soccer

Association (USYSA), U.S. Club Soccer and American Youth Soccer Organization (AYSO).

This is not the place to explore the history of why there are three organizations and not one.

Suffice it say that youth football is the key to the future. The consensus is that despite all the good they represent and all the achievements of youth football generally, the overall climate amongst the three organizations is not good (in essence, they compete against one another) and the result for the country as a whole is a pipeline of talent that is working for the women on the local and world stage, but is not working for the men either locally or globally.

Youth football in the USA is working at cross-purposes. U.S. Soccer is being pressured on a number of fronts to "rationalize" the processes and the relationships amongst the three groups (in particular where they overlap geographically), with an eye to improving both the men's and the women's game, but as we have concluded there are forces external to the football pyramid pressuring U.S. Soccer to either drag its decision-making feet or to be obstructionist.

An entire book could be written about the challenges and the proposed solutions for youth football.

In the second follow-on edition to The Football Manifesto, we will offer a concrete proposal for change.

A hint: the #1 sport in Brazil is not football. The #1 sport in Brazil is futsal.

6.5 Why Equal Pay for the USWNT is the Only Solution

Before exploring in some detail why there is such a discrepancy between the performance of the women and the men on the world stage, it is important to state the official position of The Football Manifesto regarding equal pay in the context of the USWNT and the USMNT.

With three World Cup Championships and four Olympic gold medals, if this country has even a semblance of a meritocracy left it in, then the women should be paid at least what the men get, if not more. There is no excuse for unequal pay at the national team level. This would be true irrespective of the budgetary surplus at U.S. Soccer. There should be no aspect of the treatment of the men that is different for the women – from travel and accommodations to healthcare benefits and from per diems to payments for winning, tying and losing. Everything should be the same.

That should be our message to ourselves and to the world. We recognize that the women's movement globally differs depending on the geography and culture and it may take years or longer for certain parts of the world to catch up (including FIFA itself), but the resolve and intent to create a balanced playing field for women in every sense has to be part and parcel of the philosophy of football in the USA.

No one is asking anyone to ignore the realities of capitalism. Nevertheless, it is within the confines of the national teams that this issue is being waged and there cannot be a compromise in any shape, form or fashion that undermines the women or the men. They must be treated equally with respect to wages and benefits.

One reason not to treat the women fairly in this respect has to do with empowerment and control.

Not paying the women equally "keeps them in their place." It also prevents them from becoming an empowered force inside football in the USA. The last thing U.S. Soccer wants is a union of the women and the men under one collective bargaining umbrella.

6.6 Why the Women Win and the Men Don't -- USMNT v. USWNT

The important thing to do at the very beginning of our discourse is to contextualize the USWNT and the USMNT.

The World Cup occurs for one month every four years (for both the men and the women). Based on this fact alone, it should be clear that any country's football priorities should be on the structure, performance and results of the professional leagues and clubs and the feeder mechanisms below the professional level. That is where the primary focus needs to be for the other three years and ten months.

The USA's football pyramid is in disarray. Some may reason that the football pyramid was not a barrier to the USWNT's performance and their winning three World Cups and four Olympic gold medals.

This observation is important, but more so because it masks the real challenge before us, which is the relation of the pyramid to the USMNT.

The problem today with the USMNT is that the degree of improvement since 1994 is marginal at best, and at worst we have made no progress or have fallen behind football's global leaders.

Since 1994, there have been a number of "name" players on the USMNT squad (names which have only marginal recognition outside the United States). In the nearly quarter of a century since 1994, the USA has produced one world-class on-field (non-goalee) player – Christian Pulisic (we will not address the case of Jonathan Gonzalez here).

We must not distort Christian Pulisic's accomplishments (it is much too early for that), but he is starting for a top-tier Bundesliga team in Borussia Dortmund. That fact alone is unprecedented. The fact that we cannot point to many players like him is the problem.

The USA still has not produced one male player who could command a world-class top-tier salary and a starting position on any of the world's best club football squads.

This is an indictment not of any one particular aspect of the pyramid, but of the pyramid as a whole. Given the diversity of the United States, the wealth distribution and the existing infrastructure there is no excuse for the paltry performance of the men's talent pipeline.

The USMNT of 1994 as a Benchmark

The USMNT has not made progress when compared to the team from 1994.

The failure to qualify for World Cup 2018 in Trinidad & Tobago was symptomatic of a larger problem. Disturbingly, that problem is not new. Football is a ball skills sport (we will return to this theme over and over again) and the men's pipeline we have today in the USA is not producing world-class ball skills.

The best example is the Argentina-USA game during the Copa América Centenário tournament in 2016. Argentina won 4-0.

The score is not the issue. The issue is that for 90 minutes the USA did not have one shot on goal. Not one.

Argentina is a perennial global power, and they field in Messi one of the greatest players in the history of the game.

Excuses will be found – the USA's roster was lacking a key center-forward here or a mid-fielder there or a defender, possibly due to injury.

Whatever the excuse, the pipeline in the USA should be producing sufficient talent at every position so as to be competitive with any nation in the world, and to be capable of beating any nation in the world. That is not happening.

Major League Soccer (MLS) is an affirmative action league. Affirmative action is fine if the institutions involved in supporting that policy set a global standard of excellence. MLS does not adhere to, much less strive for a global standard of excellence – its current standard and the standard it has maintained since its inception over two decades ago is the same – mediocrity.

MLS, a league whose 2018 salary cap per team is USD 4.035 million (it was USD 1.6 million when the league was founded in 1996), is not going to produce players sufficiently skilled to win a World Cup.

And U.S. Soccer is not politically or institutionally positioned to change the current state of affairs. U.S. Soccer is an integral part of the very problem that needs solving.

Why the Women Win and the Men Don't

In truth, the only on-field global standard of excellence that the USA can point to is the USWNT. Their 2015 World Cup campaign and their spectacular performance in the final (which garnered the largest TV rating of any football game in U.S. history, men or women) is testament to more than two decades at the top (or near it) of the world rankings.

When we ask what did MLS contribute to the USWNT, the answer is not much. Possibly nothing. However, one could argue that by keeping the game alive at the pro level for the men, MLS has maintained the flame alight, and this in turn has helped the women's game. Concretely, however, and statistically, MLS's contribution to the women's game is very difficult to measure.

Everyone knows that the women did not win the World Cup in 2015 (or any World Cup or Olympic medals for that matter) by relying on a thriving foundation of a massively successful women's league in the USA and Canada.

Which begs the question -- why can't the men do the same? Why can't the men win a World Cup without having a world-class league?

The answer is very simple. On the men's side there is too much global competition.

The global standard of excellence is too high. Only with sustained training, intensive on-field practices and professional games at the highest level day-in and day-out, can any country hope to field a competitive men's team to win the World Cup. And by the way, it isn't enough to win it once. To establish a global powerhouse reputation in this sport, you need to have won the World Cup several times.

The USA has no reason or justification to have swagger. Much less be arrogant.

Outside of staging the 1994 World Cup, which was admittedly a resounding success, we have contributed little or nothing to the men's game on the field.

Even our women, who are clearly world class, get scant attention, much less funding and media coverage unless it is a World Cup or Olympic year.

Lamentably, for the other three years and 10 months until the next World Cup (or the next Olympic Games), the women will be marginalized -- marginalized financially, in terms of pay, media coverage and exposure, and marginalized in terms of their very own global standard of excellence, because the league they play in, NWSL, and the clubs they play for in the USA, fail repeatedly to translate into any meaningful form of monetization. NWSL is subsidized by the football federations of the USA, Canada and Mexico. Without that subsidy, we would bear witness to a third failed women's league in the USA and Canada.

Interestingly, one obvious question to be asked is this: if the USWNT is stocked with women who are world-class and who trained for years in our youth system and then refined their skill sets in the NCAA (almost without exception), why can't the men do the same?

One theory says that if MLS paid wages to compete globally, that would transform not only the professional league at the top of the pyramid, but the entirety of the pyramid itself – from the NCAA to youth.

That theory carries no weight, based on our arguments here about rebranding strategies and business models. Simply paying more will not solve the problem.

The U.S. women have developed their skills along the years through a system and via infrastructure that is world-class when compared to women in the rest of the world. No other country in the world has an NCAA.

Europe, particularly Western Europe, has the equivalent of an integrated club system, which has global standard of excellence professional men's teams at the top of the pyramid, which in turn support (financially) professional women's teams and the youth teams and infrastructure (training facilities, coaching, etc.) below (Sweden it should be mentioned has a world-class independent women's league, without any real support from the men's league).

By way of comparison, the USA women are getting at least the same attention, support and infrastructure as their best competitors in Europe, Latin America and Asia, and in many cases it is better or the best in the world.

However, this should come with a caveat. The USA has not been able to sustain a women's professional league to match the best professional women's leagues in Europe, and this is for a very simple reason. Because those leagues in Europe in large measure, are built on top of or alongside successful men's leagues and clubs, and a well-organized pyramid below.

The women of Europe usually play under the same club brand as the men (there are exceptions of course). But if you look at the most recent UEFA women's tournament, big name clubs represented by women are the norm.

NWSL isn't quite there yet, and I would argue that NWSL will never get there under our current system.

Our professional game in the USA and Canada is fragmented and dysfunctional.

Given the difference in pay and in the quality of play in Europe, a number of the members of the USWNT are opting to play in Europe.

Irrespective of the lawsuits and other distractions that the women face, and given the pipeline of the talented women coming through the youth and NCAA pipeline, there is no reason to think otherwise, than that the USWNT will maintain their position on top of the world for the indefinite future.

We cannot say the same thing about the men. They are stuck. And the key to unlocking their potential is to recognize that the USA does not have a true Division I league by any legitimate global standard of excellence.

This fact needs to be admitted as a first step. The second thing that needs to be admitted and dealt with is that MLS will never be that league.

What is going on with the sport of football in the USA today is a form of corruption. It may not be a statutory crime, but it is at least a moral crime and an affront to football fans everywhere.

When football administrators in the United States hold themselves out as full-time dedicated servants of the game of football and full-time supporters of the fans and what is best for the game, and then betray that trust due to obligations that stem from another sport, that is corruption.

Equal pay for women at the USWNT is not a solution. That is the minimum women and everyone must demand (and go on strike if necessary to get it).

Unequal pay is a symptom of a much more serious institutional compromise. Football in the United States has been undermined. It has been subverted and the subversion continues to this day. This corruption has been hidden.

It has been masked by the very administrators of the sport who are handmaidens for another sport and another set of priorities that have nothing to do with football.

This corruption dashes the dreams of the young and their families that spend hundreds of hours on the road and thousands of dollars per year per child in pursuit of a dream.

Today, that dream can only be realized in Europe and that is the worst part of the corruption.

Striving for the USA to be #1 in the world, is about being able to dream right here in the United States of America. This is exactly the mandate of The Football Manifesto.

In its own special way, this kind of corruption is just as sinister as the misdeeds being prosecuted by the DOJ and its prosecutorial equivalent in Switzerland against FIFA officials.

The corruption is a hidden agenda. A hidden agenda to keep the sport in the USA from becoming what it could be, and what it naturally tends to be in the greatest country in the world.

This hidden agenda is there to quite literally bar, block, obstruct and eliminate whenever and wherever possible the global standard of excellence from arising – particularly from the grassroots up.

The idea behind this corruption is to maintain the USA as is, in the firmament of world football – namely, as a colony of Europe to be exploited in a 21st century version of the past. A colony to be exploited by the most powerful clubs of European football (in our summer months), but also and more importantly, as a colony that is kept in check so as not be a threat to the entrenched sports establishment of the USA, particularly the NFL.

The current closed system is in a word anti-American. It is anti-entrepreneurial, anti-grassroots, and is simply about maintaining a closed mediocre billionaire boy's club. We have nothing against billionaires, but they too can learn to survive and compete in an open football system that fully embraces the global standard of excellence.

[1] *The Case of the Cosmos.* The Cosmos brand is arguably one of the best recognized brands in the sport in the USA. That, however, is the problem. The Cosmos have never been able to translate that brand

into meaningful and sustainable revenue on a world-class scale, and this fact is applicable to both the original Cosmos and the recent reincarnation of the Cosmos.

At some point making the connection that a club's brand must resonate with the fans and community at a deeper psychic level than has previously been achieved, and in turn must be married with a radically different business model than has previously been applied in the USA, has to be addressed.

Even if we adjust for inflation, the mid-1970s value of the dollar created in the original Cosmos a glorified version of a current MLS franchise full of (exceptional) Beckham Rule players. It was not a business model or a branding strategy that was sustainable then, nor is it sustainable much less desirable today.

The insistence in believing that the Cosmos brand has sufficient value to serve as a triggering mechanism to create a world-class football club along the lines of Real Madrid, Barcelona or Manchester United is the simultaneous failure and refusal to recognize the core principles of what is wrong with football in the USA.

This same analysis is applicable to the vintage version and the current version of the NASL.

There are other football club brands in and for the New York City metropolitan area that are waiting to be discovered. Coupled with the right business model and

New York City will have the world-class club it deserves. A football club to rival any of the best clubs in Europe and Latin America.

The Case of the SF Deltas. The SF Deltas were formed in 2015 and began playing in the North American Soccer League (NASL) in the 2017 season. They won the NASL Championship in November of 2017.

It would be reasonable to assume that in the annals of men's professional football in the USA, no first year legitimate professional club has ever won a national championship -- at least in modern times. And of course in theory, if the USA had a promotion and relegation format at the professional level, the SF Deltas would be playing in MLS or some other first division league for the 2018 season.

No doubt with Pro/Rel the prospect of first division rewards (think of the 5 revenue drivers of football clubs), would have been sufficient for the SF Deltas to receive a capital increase from existing investors or from new investors anticipating the additional revenues (and returns on investment) and costs from participating in the first division.

Lamentably, that is not the case, because the SF Deltas are now defunct.

The investors in SF Deltas, led by a seasoned Silicon Valley entrepreneur and several other successful Valley investors (along with investment from Brazil) decided to pull the plug on the venture because they could not see a way to stem the accumulated losses nor forestall the continuation of such losses into the future. Sound familiar? This is the very dilemma being faced by MLS.

The difference that makes all the difference, however, is that the MLS business model is precisely structured for exactly this set of circumstances (losses in perpetuity), while the NASL business model is not. NASL in its second incarnation has, as we have previously observed, done little or nothing to distinguish itself from the original NASL – hence the applicability of the Einstein quote.

Based on the research and analysis herein it should be clear that neither business model represents a viable route to the future, much less a viable route toward the USA becoming #1 in the world of football, but in terms of long-term survivability there is no question that the MLS business model is superior to the NASL model.

With respect to branding in a Reddit Ask Me Anything (AMA) session in February 2017, the SF Delta's Founder and CEO Brian Andrés Helmick wrote: "DELTA means CHANGE. In the city of change and innovation, our goal is to take risks and grow the world's sport for fans in the entire Bay Area." The SF Delta administrative team explored the following eight (8) criteria as the foundation that led to the choice of the name Deltas: "(1) No animals, as there are too many animal team names; (2) Don't copy European club soccer in terms of naming, be original; (3) Europe is known for crests and nobility, but the USA is not; (4) With 40% of the people living in San Francisco not being born in the USA, the name should be pronounceable in most languages (e.g. "th" doesn't exist in Spanish, Portuguese, Italian, French, etc.); (5) Less is more, don't make it complicated; (6) Take risks and be different, SF is all about taking risks and being different; (7) Don't manufacture history, own the fact that you're a new team, pick a name and let your actions develop your brand and not your colors, font type, design, etc; (8) Don't over-explain things, let fans create their own relationship with the club for their own reasons." (Source: SF Deltas and Wikipedia)

There is no question that San Francisco and the Bay Area in general are destined to have not one but several top-tier fooball clubs by any global standard of excellence. The branding strategy of the Deltas didn't break the surface of the potential that is embedded in the cultural fabric of the Bay Area.

The Football Manifesto has emphasized the need for a new branding strategy *and* a new business model approach for football as a precondition to world-class league and club status. Suffice it to say that neither the NASL, the Cosmos nor the SF Deltas nor any other NASL team (past or present) satisfied those preconditions. We cannot devote more space to this issue in the context of NASL and the teams that have failed in that league or migrated to some other league (e.g., to USL or MLS). We will demonstrate this different strategy in the second edition of The Football Manifesto with the launch of a new football league and clubs and for the first time, a true football culture.

CHAPTER 7: CURRENT STATE OF THE REST OF THE WORLD

As we go to press, the four largest countries in the world by population, China (1.37 billion), India (1.26 billion), the United States of America (325 million) and Indonesia (258 million) cannot be considered global football powers (in the context of the men's game), despite the fact that these four countries represent 44% of the world's population of 7.32 billion.

7.1 The Men

Let's clarify what we mean. These four countries and the rest of the entire planet compose a strong global fan base for men's football. During the World Cup and also in off-World Cup years (largely based on the global transmission of European leagues and UEFA sponsored championships), football fans are ardently supporting the sport.

Some of the largest support networks for some of Europe's leading football clubs can be found in Asia (e.g., Manchester United is very popular in China).

What we mean by not being a football power, therefore, is focused on the men's game and means (i) not having a successful track record at competing in World Cup Finals competitions and in regional and global club competitions, and (ii) not having a globally competitive professional league and fully integrated youth development program.

Of the four most populous nations in the world, India has never participated in a Men's World Cup Finals (excluding qualifying rounds). Indonesia and China have both appeared once, respectively as the Dutch East Indies (in 1950) and China in 2002. Of the 20 World Cups to date, the USA has played in 10, having qualified for every World Cup since 1990 until the debacle of 2017 in Trinidad & Tobago. The highest finish of the USA was third place in 1930.

Of the 20 men's World Cups 11 have been won by European countries, and 9 have been won by South American countries.

7.2 The Women

There have been 7 Women's World Cup Finals beginning in 1991. The USA has won 3 World Cup titles, followed by Germany (2) and Norway and Japan (1 each). The USA hosted the tournament in 1999 and 2003. The USWNT has also won 4 Olympic gold medals in football.

The German women, in addition to their WC championships in 2003 and 2007, have one runners-up and two fourth place finishes in WC competition. There have been six Olympic football competitions for women. The German women have three third place bronze medal finishes and one gold medal championship (2016).

If the USA were to emulate one country in terms of creating a world-class football program for men and women, it would have to be Germany.

Japan appears to be in the midst of a new generation of exceptional players having won the women's WC in 2011 and been runners-up in 2015.

Importantly, China hosted two of those World Cups (1991 and 2007) and finished in 4th place in 1995 and as runners-up in 1999 (both in a field of 16). On the women's side, therefore, China is a legitimate force as well.

Norway (along with its WC championship in 1995, has a runner-up and two fourth place finishes) and Sweden (one WC runners-up and two third-place finishes) are always in the running.

Brazil's women are noteworthy for having produced some of the best individual talent that the sport has seen (men or women), but they have yet to win a major FIFA-sponsored tournament. The team finished the 1999 World Cup in third place and the 2007 World Cup in second, losing to Germany in the final, 2–0. Brazil won the silver medal twice at the Olympics in 2004 and 2008, after getting fourth place in the two previous Olympics.

India and Indonesia are still working for their place in the women's game.

On the club side of the equation for women, the four most populous countries are still in the early stages of development. Only Europe has world-class club competition for women, with Sweden a particular club competition stand-out.

The purpose of this publication is to focus on the other 3 years and 10 months between World Cup competitions. And within that context, our primary focus is on the USA.

Even so, everything written here should be applicable, with adjustments for culture and legal frameworks, to not only China, India and Indonesia, but to any country in the world.

The immediate intention is for the second edition of this publication is become the go-to reference and source on how to structure, manage and grow a football league, football clubs and a football culture in your village, town, city, region or country.

Most of what is discussed here in terms of branding/marketing, business models, football clubs and the creation of football culture, is borrowed from proven strategies and experiences in the USA, Europe and Latin America, the latter two regions of the world where football is strongest.

PART III: FUTURE STATE OF FOOTBALL IN THE USA

In speaking about the future of football in the USA after Carlos Cordeiro's election in February 2018, let's return again to a global perspective:

"They need to bring in a football culture to the whole country . . . As FIFA President, I have to care about having also challengers to the European associations and leagues."
--- Gianni Infantino, FIFA President, in an ESPN interview the week after the U.S. Soccer elections.

The Football Manifesto is about *creating that football culture in the USA.*

The Football Manifesto is also about *creating in the USA those challengers to the European associations and leagues.*

No country as large as the United States, both in land area and population – and no country as rich or as demographically diverse as the United States has become a global football power.

This section of The Football Manifesto is about the VISION.

The FUTURE STATE lays down the parameters of what the future will be like when the VISION for The

Football Manifesto and Club Handbook has been realized.

2025: VISION USA

- 32 CLUB FIRST DIVISION
- 32 CLUB SECOND DIVISION
- LEAGUE REVENUE AT USD 8 BILLION
- 4 CLUBS IN THE DELOITTE FOOTBALL MONEY LEAGUE (FML)
- PROMOTION & RELEGATION
- LOWER PROFESSIONAL DIVISIONS STRUCTURED
- TOP OF THE PYRAMID FULLY INTEGRATED WITH THE BOTTOM OF THE PYRAMID
- FANS AS MEMBER-OWNERS OF FOOTBALL CLUBS
- PLAYERS AS MEMBER-OWNERS OF FOOTBALL CLUBS
- MEMBER-OWNERS AS HIGH NET WORTH INDIVIDUALS AND HUNDREDS OF THOUSANDS OF CLUB MEMBERS
- STADIA – AT LEAST TEN (10) DIVISION I SIZE STADIA (50,000 AND UP)
- WOMEN & MEN – PLAYING UNDER THE SAME CLUB BRAND
- FOOTBALL CLUBS AS 24/7 COMMUNITY RESOURCES

- FOOTBALL CLUB BRANDS – NEW BRANDS TO RIVAL THE BEST CLUB BRANDS OF EUROPE AND LATIN AMERICA
- GOVERNANCE – TOP DOWN & BOTTOM UP
- REVENUE DRIVERS – ALL 5 AT MAXIMUM PRODUCTION
- SALARY CAP – GLOBALLY COMPETITIVE
- PLAYER CONTRACTS – BOSMAN RULE FOR THE AMERICAS

PART IV: TRANSITION STATE – HOW TO GET FROM TODAY TO #1 IN THE WORLD

"Artur Friedenreich, son of a German immigrant and a black washerwoman, played in the first division for twenty-six years and never earned a cent. No one scored more goals than he in the history of soccer, not even that other great Brazilian artilleryman, Pelé, who remains professional soccer's leading scorer. Freidenreich accumulated 1,329, Pelé 1,279. The green-eyed mulatto founded the Brazilian style of play. He, or the devil who got into him through the sole of his foot, broke all the rules in the English manuals: Friedenreich brought to the solemn stadium of the whites the irreverence of brown boys who entertained themselves fighting over a rag ball in the slums. Thus was born a style open to fantasy, one which prefers pleasure to results. From Friedenreich onward, there have been no right angles in Brazilian soccer, just as there are none in the mountains of Rio de Janeiro or the buildings of Oscar Niemeyer."
--- Eduardo Galeano on the evolution of Brazilian football.

"My model for business is The Beatles. They were four guys who kept each other's kind of negative tendencies in check. They balanced each other and the total was greater than the sum of the parts. That's

how I see business: great things in business are never done by one person, they're done by a team of people."
--- Steve Jobs

Putting the Challenge of Becoming #1 in the World in Perspective

When we assume the mantle of wanting to be #1 in the world it changes things.

One of the assumptions that fans of football have assumed for decades is that U.S. Soccer would solve things – that somehow the football pyramid would be rationalized and restructured.

This book is bringing you some news – U.S. Soccer will not build this house for you. You have to build it!

The purpose of The Football Manifesto is to provide blueprints and tools to help you do just that.

One of the key aspects of this new set of blueprints is the concept of the football club.

The most difficult thing to imagine is *having the equivalent* of Real Madrid, Barcelona, Manchester United, Manchester City, Chelsea, Tottenham, Bayern Münich, PSG, etc. in the USA and Canada.

So let us trigger your imagination a bit.

According to worldometers.info the Big 5 countries of Europe have a population of 318,989,578, while the USA and Canada combined have a population of 361,083,662.

Here is the country-by-country breakdown – The Big 5: Germany (82,114,224), U.K. (66,181,585), France (64,979,548), Italy (59,359,900) and Spain (46,354,321), and the USA (324,459,463) and Canada (36,624,199).

According to FIFA nearly one person in every 25 of the world's population of 7+ billion plays football. In the CONCACAF region that ratio rises to one in 12 people, the highest amongst the six confederations.

In addition, women participating in football (about 1/10 of the total) is higher in CONCACAF than in any other confederation. Approximately two percent of the world's population are women playing the game in North and Central America and the Caribbean, which is almost ten times the number in each of the other five confederations.

In terms of registered players (again according to FIFA) the USA has 4,186,778 and Canada has 865,712. Amongst the Big 5 football powers of Europe we have registered players in Germany at 6,308,945, France with 1,794,940, Italy with 1,513,596, the U.K. with 1,485,910, and Spain with 653,190. The Big 5 together have 11,753,582 registered players.

Based on its population and the goal of becoming #1, the USA should establish a target of 16,000,000 registered players. This may seem daunting. It isn't. The USA has over 20 million non-registered players. All that needs to be done is get one half of them to sign up and participate in building a football nation and a football culture.

That is imminently doable in this age of social media. We just need to tell them a new story.

That new story is what The Football Manifesto is all about.

Putting Professional Football in the USA in Perspective

Lastly, we have the question of clubs. FIFA claims (no doubt via U.S. Soccer) that the USA has 9,000 clubs. Canada has 10,000. With 1/10 the population Canada has more clubs than the USA.

Again according to FIFA, Germany has 26,837 clubs, Brazil has 29,208 clubs, Argentina has 3,377 clubs, Italy has 16,697 clubs, France 20,062 clubs, the U.K. 42,490 clubs, Spain 18,190 clubs.

The USA and Canada have a good foundation to build on. But build we must.

The total number of clubs in the Big 5 football powers of Europe combined is 124,276 clubs. Those five countries are roughly equal to the population of the USA.

If we take the Big 5 (the EPL, the Bundesliga, La Liga, Serie A and Ligue 1) together we have 98 top-tier first division clubs from Europe.

If we add in the second division of each of those leagues we add another 106 clubs for a total of 204 clubs comprising the best football in Europe.

Right now the USA has no football club that can compete day-in day-out at either level.

So in the USA when everyone is clamoring for promotion and relegation, with the obvious emphasis on promotion (because this is the battle cry of those below MLS), the real question is "promoted to what?"

MLS?

Let's quit kidding ourselves and get serious!

Part of the exercise of creating new clubs in the USA and Canada is acknowledging that to become truly world-class, to become #1 in the world, we will have to create *at least* a dozen or more clubs that can compete on the level of the best clubs in the first division leagues of Europe and Latin America.

We will also need to create two to three dozen clubs that can compete with the best of Europe and Latin America's second divisions.

As it stands, U.S. Soccer-MLS/SUM has created the football we have today and maintained it for 20+ years, but they have also knocked football off of its feet.

Football is lying prone on its back and unconscious in the USA and Canada.

It's time to bring out the smelling salts!!!   It is time to wake up!!!

It is time to create a football culture!!!

Stop kidding yourselves about what U.S. Soccer-MLS/SUM is going to do.

Get over it. You have been burned. Your lover is sleeping with someone else.

It is time to get your life in order!!! Get some therapy (this book), get some exercise (study what a football nation and a football culture means) and then go and build something (football clubs)!!!

Bringing a Football Club to Your Corner of the Universe

Your purchase of this book and your contributions to Patreon will go toward the creation of the second edition of The Football Manifesto.

In that second edition, we will be providing you with an A to Z Toolkit for all of your football club formation needs.

The second edition will be a one-stop shop for all of your legal, design, marketing, technology, real estate and financing requirements, as well as fan outreach, recruitment and retention. This will include training and supervision about how to operate a democratic fan and/or community-driven member-owned football club.

In addition, the second edition will include feedback mechanisms and a platform that will grow to fully nurture our individual and collective efforts to reach our goal of the USA becoming #1 in the world.

Also, and most importantly, as a part of that second edition, The Football Manifesto and Club Handbook will be launching a new professional football league and sixteen new football clubs using the fan member-owner model. These clubs are being structured to compete on a par with the best clubs in Europe and Latin America. The new football club brands will compete directly with the best football club brands from around the world.

Brazil Should Be the USA's Global Benchmark for On-Field Excellence

In terms of land area, population size and demographic mix, Brazil is the country in the world most like the USA.

Football and demographics in the USA set the stage for a new football model from a branding and business model perspective.

In particular, the USA's inner-city cultural milieu that has been largely on the periphery of football, presents the key factors at the essence of what is needed for a football culture. In this sense, the USA is a diamond in the rough. Our job now is to polish it.

Brazil is the largest black country outside of Africa. It is estimated that anywhere from 7 to 10 times as many slaves were brought to Brazil as to the United States. Of Brazil's population of 205 million well over 50% of the population is considered black or of mixed African blood.

By way of comparison of the 325 million people in the United States, roughly 13% or some 42 million are considered African-American or black. Even so, 75% of the players in the NBA are African-American, while nearly 70% of the players in the NFL are.

In addition, and just as crucially in terms of importance, are statistics related to the USA's Hispanic population. There are 56 million Hispanics in the USA, with

Mexico representing 63.3% of that total according to the most recent Pew Research Center study. As we have mentioned, Los Angeles is the second largest Spanish-speaking city in the world (Mexico City is #1). There are more than 1 million people of Mexican origin in Chicago and there are more Spanish speaking people in the USA than Spain's entire population. The majority of Hispanics in the USA come from cultures where football is the dominant sport. To say they "get" football culture is an understatement. They *are* football culture.

As already mentioned, St. Louis has the largest concentration of Bosnians outside of Bosnia and to refer back to Chicago, Chicago also has the largest population of Polish descendants outside of Poland, a population of over 1 million from a rabid football culture.

The USA and Canada have dozens of metropolitan areas with populations that are ethnically and culturally diverse, with representation from Europe, Africa, Latin America and Asia.

By bringing all of the USA's and Canada's ethnic populations fully under the football umbrella we can become #1 in the world. Without bringing literally all of these groups together, we will not make it. The effort to become #1 in the world has to be about inclusion. Total inclusion has to be the mantra.

While Asians and Native Americans have not had major impacts as players in the dominant sports practiced in the USA (including football), they nevertheless represent important, even crucial parts of our cultural mosaic and must be fully included in the creation of this new wave of creating a football culture. Bobby Wood is just the beginning.

Why are these demographic trends relevant to our discussion about football and particularly football culture?

For three (3) reasons.

First, the penetration to date that football has in the USA's inner-cities is paltry. There are many who would rather ignore the athletic statistics and accomplishments, but it is a classic understatement to say that some of the greatest athletes on this planet have come from inner-city neighborhoods in the United States. If the USA is serious about becoming a world-class football power, black, Hispanic, Asian, Native American and European ethnic groups and their rural, suburban and inner-city athletic talent must be *fully* tapped into.

Second, and just as importantly, inner-city culture (particularly black inner-city culture, which increasingly overlaps with Hispanic culture) has evolved to become a global cultural force impacting design, fashion, music, art and I will argue here, potentially football. To reformulate this, we have the raw materials to create what the USA has never had – a compelling football culture.

The foundation for that culture already exists in new hip-hop trends, contemporary offshoots of graffiti/design, and a phenomenon called *tanning* – a concept introduced by Steve Stoute's VH-1 video series and book called the *Tanning of America*.

To reiterate, *Tanning* is a phenomenon that reflects the melding together of racial, religious and cultural backgrounds, often with a youth-focused undercurrent of urban, hip-hop and cultural creatives across a digitized network of global villages.

It is a process of inclusion not exclusion. It is also a reflection of a deep tribal connection across our species.

Tanning has to do with *interior mental landscapes*. We can all be tan.

No two countries are better positioned to exploit the *tanning* of football globally, than the United States and Canada.

The next great harvest of football club brands that have global impact will be created in the United States and Canada and it will be inner-city culture and *tanning* that drives their creation.

Some of these new brands will draw and monetize from a local or regional fan base, or even a national one, but the best of these new brands will monetize via a global fan base.

In the chapter on branding, we explained that a brand with strong local and/or regional appeal to be a Tier 3 brand. A new brand that has appeal nationally is a Tier 2 brand. And a new brand that generates a local, national *and* global following is a Tier 1 brand.

Think of New York City, Los Angeles, Chicago, Toronto and other melting pot cities where cross-cultural and cross-generational melding is the norm. These metropolitan areas will produce some of the great Tier 1 and Tier 2 football club brands in this new vision for professional football.

The process of discovering these new brands requires an unprecedented plunge into the collective psychic, cultural and historical depths of the United States' and Canada's evolving demographics, history and culture. It is there that we find the essence of football's *tanning and branding potential*. It is there that we will create the bedrock of a football culture.

The argument for rebranding football is based on one simple fact. Football is more than a sport -- it is a culture.

Rebranding is a realization that there is another deeper level of cultural connectedness, which has no precedent in the world of professional sports in the United States and Canada.

This deeper level unites us, triggers our collective passions and importantly has not been fully tapped into in terms of its commercial potential.

Third and last, Brazil's size (it is larger than the 48 states of the United States), demographic mix of indigenous, African, European, Asian populations (São Paulo is the largest Japanese city outside of Japan) and the culture around the sport of football that resulted, coupled with Brazil's global accomplishments on the field (the only 5 time FIFA World Cup Champion), makes it the prime example and the principal bar to be reached by the USA as a global standard of on-field excellence. Brazil continues to be the global standard bearer for *futebol arte*.

Germany Should be the Benchmark for Off-Field Football League Structure and Administration

Aside from being the highest attended football league on the planet at roughly 42,000 a game, Germany is the quintessential nation for fan and community-owned football clubs. In addition, the Bundesliga (both Divisions 1 and 2) has some of the highest professional standards being applied to league and club administration.

The most recent Bundesliga report for the 2016-17 campaign, indicates that Germany broke its record for revenue generated at better than 3 billion Euros for the first division, and just over a half a billion Euros for the second division. That is more than USD 3.5 billion in revenue between the two divisions of 18 clubs each.

Even more impressively, sixteen of the eighteen Bundesliga clubs in the first division earned a profit. On the basis of EBITDA (earnings before interest, taxes, depreciation and amortization) all eighteen clubs were in the black. If both leagues were viewed together thirty-four of the thirty-six were profitable, as was the case in the prior year.

Given the fan and community ownership structure, this is proof that it can be done.

The challenge for the USA, however, is different. Football in the USA is facing competition from other leisure and entertainment options, including the Big 4, and it is also facing opposition from its own football federation and first division professional league (which have been corrupted).

With a population of 82 million, Germany is roughly 1/4 the size of the USA in population. In order for a new model to be introduced into the USA it must scale to nationwide impact. Think 4 Germanys.

So from an on-field performance perspective the goal is for the USA to emulate Brazil, and from the standpoint of off-field performance and organization the USA should emulate Germany (for both the men and the women). Those are the two global standards of excellence being promoted by The Football Manifesto.

If you believe other countries hold out better examples of on-field and/or off-field performance feel free to trumpet their virtues. The one thing we cannot do is compromise the global standard of excellence.

In summary, the TRANSITION STATE consists of the following (which will be fully embodied in the strategic plan and launch of the new professional league and clubs in the second edition of The Football Manifesto):

Instead of:

- A top-down approach, a bottom-up + a top-down approach
- Soccer teams, football clubs
- Fans as consumers, fans as member-owners
- Teams owned by a few billionaires, clubs owned by hundreds of thousands
- A day at the stadium, a 24/7 football club as a community resource
- Old soccer team names, new football club brands to rival the best from Europe and Latin America
- A low salary cap, a globally competitive salary cap
- Stadium receipts as the principal driver of revenue, all five (5) revenue drivers at maximum
- The Beckham Rule, a Bosman Rule for the Americas

- Old stars, young stars
- Women and men in separate leagues, women and men under the same club brand
- Division III stadia, Division I stadia
- A closed system, an open system
- No promotion & relegation, promotion & relegation

CLOSING REMARKS AND NEXT STEPS

We are at the end of the road as far as the first edition of The Football Manifesto is concerned.

And yet, this is just the beginning. A new football story has begun and this time it is being written by those who have the beautiful game at heart. All of us are the authors.

The second edition of The Football Manifesto will reinforce the launch of this new era, with a new football league and clubs that will fill a void at the top of the football pyramid in the USA.

Everyone should be looking forward to becoming member-owners of the first set of football clubs – football clubs that will establish the global standard of excellence on the field and off.

"Those who fail to know history are condemned to repeat it."
--- George Santayana

The era of fake news began long ago. It is not something that appeared on the scene post-Obama. Not knowing history is part of the challenge – because the history we have been told has been manufactured for our consumption. True history requires self-inspection. It requires dealing with the lies we have told ourselves. And the lies we have been fed.

After that the only requirement is constant vigilance.

The Football Manifesto begins the process of dealing with reality and dealing with truth and deconstructing the false history and false promises we have been sold.

For it is capitalism's negative side and its pure unbridled self-interest that has led to U.S. Soccer-MLS/SUM becoming mere instruments of the NFL and to a commensurate extent, UEFA-FIFA. The heavy lifting of this ruse about football and its future in the USA was done and is still being done by the NFL and their anointed minions. The days of the pied pipers who wear two hats are over.

We need to be able to separate with eyes wide open, the individuals from the institutions. There are some good solid people working inside and at all levels of the football pyramid.

These good people once identified need an alternative institutional framework to work with for football's future.

That alternative institutional framework is what the second edition of The Football Manifesto is all about.

Certain institutions can be reformed. U.S. Soccer as currently structured is not one of them. It has become the electoral college of football. MLS, which maintains its monopoly as a result is also not the future of football.

Each of these institutions needs to be left by the side of the road.

Meanwhile, if we want football in the USA to be #1 in the world, we must carve out a new path.

This brings to mind a poem of Robert Frost's:

The Road Not Taken

Two roads diverged in a yellow wood,
And sorry I could not travel both
And be one traveler, long I stood
And looked down one as far as I could
To where it bent in the undergrowth;

Then took the other, as just as fair,
And having perhaps the better claim,
Because it was grassy and wanted wear;
Though as for that the passing there
Had worn them really about the same,

And both that morning equally lay
In leaves no step had trodden black.
Oh, I kept the first for another day!
Yet knowing how way leads on to way,
I doubted if I should ever come back.

I shall be telling this with a sigh
Somewhere ages and ages hence:

Two roads diverged in a wood, and I—
I took the one less traveled by,
And that has made all the difference.

POSTSCRIPT

THE RECENT ELECTION FOR U.S. SOCCER'S PRESIDENT. The vote for U.S. Soccer President took place on Saturday February 10, 2018 in Orlando, Florida at the Annual General Meeting (AGM). The new president Carlos Cordeiro, who replaces Sunil Gulati, won on the third ballot with 68.6% of the vote. Kathy Carter, former head of MLS's Soccer United Marketing (SUM) came in second place in that same round with 10.6% of the vote.

The total percentage vote for the two front-running candidates, both of whom had the support of MLS was 79.2%, well over three-quarters of the voting total. In the second round, these same two candidates led the voting and had respectively 41.8% and 33.3% of the total vote for a combined 75.1% of the vote. And in the first round of voting these same two candidates led the voting and had respectively 36.3% and 34.6% of the vote for a combined 70.9% of the total vote.

Given U.S. Soccer's weighted voting procedures it is mathematically safe to assume that Kathy Carter's presence in the election is the only thing that prevented Carlos Cordeiro from winning on the first ballot. Given that both candidates had the support of MLS, it is perfectly reasonable to assume that Kathy Carter's candidacy was politically expedient – that is, in the field of eight (8) candidates, with the two leading candidates being supported by MLS, the three rounds of election results created the impression of a competitive election, when in fact the outcome had been known from the outset.

Any doubts about who controls U.S. Soccer before the election, can now be confirmed definitively, it is MLS.

Ms. Carter may have known from the very beginning that the deck was stacked against her. If that is the case, then she quite consciously resolved to play the role of candidate in a charade. If that is not the case, that is, if Ms. Carter actually thought that she had a chance to win and was told (no doubt by her sponsors at MLS) that with the support of MLS those chances were at least 50-50, then she was duped.

Interestingly, this same pattern of voting, where switching candidates post the first round proved to be politically fruitful for U.S. Soccer-MLS/SUM was last seen in the election of Gianni Infantino as President of FIFA in 2015, where the USA shifted its vote after the first round to Mr. Infantino, thereby assuring his victory.

THE USA-MEXICO-CANADA JOINT BID FOR THE 2026 WORLD CUP. Winning the WC26 Bid is both wonderful news (for those who love the sport in the USA, Mexico and Canada) and simultaneously and potentially an ominous sign for football in the USA.

If U.S. Soccer-MLS/SUM and their partners could successfully leverage and profit from the 2016 Copa América Centenário, it doesn't take much imagination to consider the money-making and profit-generating potential of WC26

WC26 Bid Chairman Carlos Cordeiro has said that the event would create a USD 11 billion profit for FIFA from total revenues of USD 14 billion. These figures, should they come to fruition, will shatter the record profit from WC18 in Russia which has been estimated to be between USD 6-7 billion.

Even considering that the USA will split some of those revenues and profits with Mexico and Canada, it is reasonable to assume given the proposed format that substantial gains will accrue to U.S. Soccer-MLS/SUM and their partners (of the 80 games, 60 will be held in the USA -- all in NFL stadia).

Given the current leadership, structure and controls of U.S. Soccer-MLS/SUM, and given the more than two decade long corrupt scheme that is maintaining football in the USA as a second or even third-tier sport domestically and globally, WC26 could become more of a threat to football than a boon.

The tendency is to maintain the status quo or a status quo that is palatable to the NFL -- using the gains from WC26 to guarantee that scenario.

Those who control football in the USA, view football as the primary threat to American football (of the NFL variety).

The Football Manifesto is about tilting the balance in favor of the people who love the beautiful game and who have dedicated their time, their energy and their money exclusively to grow the sport, along with those young men and women players who want to create and experience first-hand a real and legitimate football culture.

These people collectively, numbering in the tens of millions, deserve to be able to work unencumbered and without interference (from third-parties with other conflicting agendas) to reach the goal of the USA becoming #1 in the world of football.

We do not need WC26 to get there. What this sport needs and what those who support this sport with their hearts, minds an souls need, is for the top administrators of this sport to either step aside, or at a minimum to stop blocking progress. [1]

It all begins now, by insisting upon (i) the global standard of excellence, (ii) rebranding and restructuring the sport from top to bottom and (iii) fan and community member-owned and controlled football clubs.

With the changes proposed in The Football Manifesto, the USA will be well on its way to becoming #1 by WC26!!!

[1] Chapter 6: U.S. Soccer's War speaks to exactly this issue -- an undermining of the game by the very officials who administer the sport. In addition to the facts communicated in Chapter 6 we have a new development. This time the problem is focused on youth football at the grassroots level in our inner-cities.

The U.S. Soccer Foundation, a 501c3 not-for-profit corporation, separate and apart and not controlled by U.S. Soccer, has plans to take the sport to 1,000,000 inner-city youth by 2026 and use WC26 as the drawing card. Since its founding in 1994 (with WC94 proceeds), the Foundation has invested over USD 125 million to improve access to football for inner-city youth, largely in low-income neighborhoods.

In response to this laudable initiative by the Foundation and after winning the rights to WC26, U.S. Soccer formally wrote to the Foundation in August 2018, announcing that it was unilaterally severing its 20+ year relationship with the Foundation and requesting the immediate devolution of the Foundation brand and all related intellectual property rights.

The U.S. Soccer Foundation response was to sue the U.S. Soccer Federation (U.S. Soccer) in federal court seeking declaratory judgment relief. Why is this happening? And why now?

Because the U.S Soccer Foundation's plan for 1,000,000 inner-city youth playing football by WC26 would interfere with the pipeline into the NFL of that same inner-city talent.

THE END